W9-ANU-375

FRIENDSHIP

Martin E. Marty

Argus Communications
A Division of DLM, Inc.
Allen, Texas 75002 U.S.A.

Cover designed by Design Office
Cover photo Jim Whitmer
Illustrations by Jesse T. Hummingbird

FIRST EDITION

© Copyright 1980 Argus Communications.

Printed in the United States of America.

Argus Communications
A Divison of DLM, Inc.
One DLM Park
Allen, Texas 75002 U.S.A.

Library of Congress Number: 80-69243
International Standard Book Number: 0-89505-053-6

To Beverly and Dean Lueking

"Holy Friendship . . . truly is [from God], that amid the wretchedness of this exile, we be comforted with the counsel of friends until we come to Him."
Richard Rolle -1349

Contents

1

Survival

We have friends, or we are friends, in order that we do not get killed.

So say some schools of scientists. They connect animal behavior with human behavior. They believe that animal ancestors of humans found it necessary to band together in order to protect themselves from other bands. These bands fought over limited food supplies, or whatever else animals fight over. The beast who stood alone stood no chance at all. No dank cave could hide him permanently. Sooner or later he would have to come to the light of morning in order to forage for food. Then others would pounce on him.

So our ancestor learned on purely strategic terms to find company. In this company he could help do the pouncing. In the course of time such practical arrangements among the animals produced an instinct much like affection. The beasts came to find company not only necessary but attractive. That sense of attraction, say our speculating scientists, was passed on by the animals as their species evolved to become *homo sapiens.* Human beings, in their turn, simply kept on finding it expedient to band together, instinctive to show affection, and finally natural to have friends and to be friends.

Such theories have as many supporters as they have enemies in the halls of science, and they probably have more enemies than defenders outside those halls. Not everyone buys the theories of descent on which such scientists base their views of the origins of friendship. Many who do share those theories say that we have no way of testing how animals became friends or how they passed their ways on to humans. And even many who buy into the notion that friendship is a trace of animal descent resist the idea that such a notion explains everything. To hear that friendship is the result of "nothing but" animal behavior does not ring true. We are creatures who live not by "nothing buttery," but by "something more."

Still, the speculators have given a clue about what it is to be or not to be friends today. For a second time, then:

We have friends, or we are friends, in order that we do not get killed.

Translate that to the modern battlefield. Enemies faced each other across the trenches in the First World War, but most fighters on each side had friends. Among the Americans they were called buddies. A buddy was not necessarily someone whom a particular soldier would have liked back home. He might have been on a rival football team. Maybe he would have competed for grades, girl friends, or

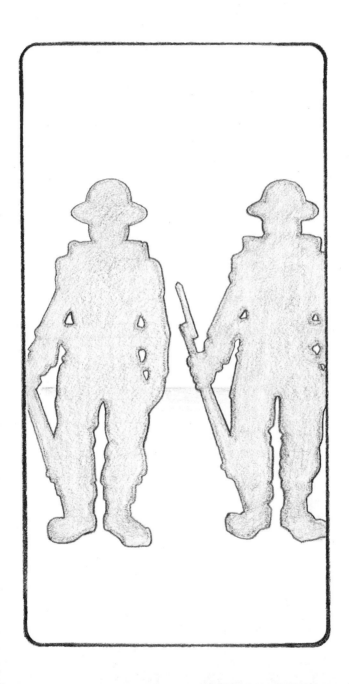

jobs. Most likely he would have been no one, a stranger far away. The first soldier would never have heard of him, never cared about him. Only the accident of the military draft brought them together.

Together now in the mud, both had to be buddies, or they would get killed. If one were thoughtless and lit a cigarette, the flicker of his match could serve as a kind of electric magnet to draw enemy fire. A buddy covered for a fellow soldier who had to slither over the lip of the trench and crawl to fulfill an assignment. Or he alerted comrades to danger. A soldier needed a buddy should he be wounded, and someone had to drag him to safety. They did each other favors, like saving each other's lives. Eventually, like the animals from whom they descended, two soldiers found that the strategy of being together paid off in something like affection. And they transformed that instinct into being friends.

So the war ended and they returned home. The two veterans found that they were not fully themselves unless they kept alive the reality of being friends. They often went fishing together. They were glad to introduce their girl friends to each other, and later their wives and children. Maybe they vacationed together. In trouble, they called upon each other. They sent Christmas cards. When their children celebrated occasions, they sent presents. They cared and cried when something went wrong in each other's circles. Finally one friend died, so something in the other one departed too. But the friend lived in memory, and that made it possible for the survivor to endure. All this began because it was once expedient and useful for a soldier to have a friend in order to stay alive in the face of killing.

World War I seems far away, but other wars and other kinds conflict keep showing how advisable it is for moderns to band together, to show a need for each other, and to seal that need by letting affection grow. But few would be content to let their friends be nothing more than part of a strategy for survival. That would be another example of "nothing buttery." The soldiers provided another clue to friendship, but they did not exhaust its meaning. For a third time:

We have friends, or we are friends, in order that we do not get killed.

Thoughtful people need conjure no cave of animals, no trench full of warriors, to see the truth of this. They only need look around in daily life, to see the killing and dying of the friendless.

You can kill a person with an apartment as well as with a machine gun. It only takes a little longer. Look closely at life in urban America, where apartments can be as dangerous as battlefield trenches. The long, straight, ugly corridors of an impersonal high-rise are not comfortable places to express the friendliness and informality that come naturally on the streets of a close-knit urban neighborhood. Transplanted from warm, familiar surroundings, inhabitants of modern housing projects may find themselves imprisoned in lonely, isolated worlds from which they can imagine no escape. Picture one case in which abandonment and neglect found the opportunity to kill.

The urban renewal program took away the little two-flat for which an old woman and her husband were making payments when he died. The planners at city hall had better ideas for the people on her

block. To the scene they sent the mortal enemies of families and friends, the bulldozers. Soon the old house was rubble. Rats came to gorge on the garbage left by the people who had lived there. Then the planners built skyscrapers that looked as stark and bare as those in Moscow. To people tunneling past on the expressway at a safe distance, these seemed neater than the old slum houses.

Up close, a patient visitor could find the old woman in one of the units. She now kept her thoughts to herself. Her neighborhood was desolate. The wreckers had leveled the friendly store when Ma and Pa, with whom she used to chat, retired. The other people who used to greet her by name when she came for groceries were now sealed off anonymously in other high-rises along the superhighway. She never saw one of them again. Oh, no, come to think of it, she once glimpsed an old man who used to ask her the time of day. He was being put into an ambulance at the door of the building just across the way. So far as she knew, he never came back.

A social worker came by every few weeks. She was friendly, but not a friend. When the old woman died, Case #024 was closed, and no trace of a person remained. No children or grandchildren existed, no friends remembered or even were told. The cars keep speeding past the rows of high-rises. Teenagers will molest other old people, the aged who have nothing to do but stare at their broken and imageless television sets between occasional furtive trips to the store. The predators will attack them on the day the Social Security check comes, or as they carry a few groceries to their apartments. The lucky ones, the crippled and the blind, are so immobile that Meals on Wheels will visit them. Each day a volunteer from the churches will stop by with a hot lunch and cold dinner. The visitor will say a friendly "Hi!" and find a piece of third-class mail to post every few weeks. The volunteer will ask whether the victim of the apartment is feeling well and has any needs. And then, despite all the good will in the world, there has to be a good-bye—other stops lie ahead. Some day all those stops will end. The ignoring city has killed persons with apartments by taking away their friends or even the possibility of friends.

We have friends, or we are friends, in order that we do not get killed.

To that sentence we added another: "You can kill a person with an apartment as well as with a machine gun." That notion, which applies to the aged and the poor victims of the city, does not end with them. There are also younger, more chic, and smarter people in the city, who foolishly allow fear and distrust to confine them to their luxury apartments.

Assaulting the skyline of the city is one of a number of glass high-rise complexes. This one has gained awards for its architecture. Bored doormen in uniform open the doors of limousines or taxicabs in which the groomed people come and go. The manager pays them to say, "Have a nice day." The residents wear gems that match the sparkle of their building against the night sky. No social worker need call on them, thank you. The only meals on wheels they see come on room service carts. Room service: a good idea. The apartment dwellers do not have to bestir themselves to go to a table for one in a cafe.

14

Wealthy people know that alone, even they can represent a problem for those who run the kinds of restaurants they patronize. Table captains shunt singles off into the shadows. Bachelors cast a pall over the tables of couples who come in parties of four or more. Tips are hardly worthwhile for waiters when only one person is eating. Room service is convenient and unembarrassing.

Being friendless in the posh high-rise does not mean having no associates. Consider a busy executive who once upon a time went to college and belonged to a fraternity. He and his buddies left the trenches of the classrooms for the no-man's-land of the rugby field, after which the bruised winners and losers showed their camaraderie by lifting cool glasses of brew. Together they had their Saturday night drunks and their Florida spring vacations. After college some of them lined up jobs at the best law firms, or gained the power to run businesses, or found spots in the media. All day long our businessman works in the company of associates who often act friendly at the Christmas party, on the last day of a Club Mediterranee vacation, or over cocktails. Then the day ends, and no party is scheduled that night. He hurries off to his glassed-in, shag-rugged cave forty stories up, nodding politely to the doorman's paid-for "Good night." On the elevator are the nameless neighbors he has greeted daily for six years. He is careful: To get acquainted is to build a bond.

If someone makes a friend, he loses some liberty and starts getting hassled. Friends have a way of inviting someone to disrupt a schedule. Sooner or later, conversation passes beyond barstool banter or cocktail party talk. Friends engage others, and want to hear their stories. They do not merely talk to hear themselves. Their hearts reach out, and that makes them dangerous.

Who knows, someday a potential friend may have a problem. Then his friends will have to become involved. One may be sick, and the other will visit. He may die, and his friend will feel the loss for years. A friend may be fickle and turn to other people. The sight of her back will come as a rebuff. Rather than take such risks, our fearful executive holes up in his apartment with his magazines. Paperback books or public television provide stories of people. These people are safe because they are fictional, living only in lines of print or as images. If they die, they do not matter. By living as fictions they help keep chaos at a distance from the reader or viewer. But they never get close enough to interrupt anyone by becoming his friends.

After the fraternity house and before the apartment hermitage, our businessman once lived in a house with his wife and two children. He remembers the children well, since he sees them every other weekend. In a way they are friends. Their mother is nice enough to teach them some friendly questions: "How are things at work?" And they have been coached in friendly suggestions: "Why don't we go to the zoo this afternoon?" (Translation: "At least we don't have to go to Sunday School in the suburbs this morning. But—ugh!—I'm sick and tired of the zoo.") So the ex-husband, busy executive, and successful planner, still a father, more or less, goes through the motions of being a friend to the kids. Once, there, for a moment around mid-afternoon, the three of them know a kind of spontaneous warmth that comes from being in the presence of people who care. It fades fast as the children argue with each other and their father tries to referee. He loses his temper and drops them off early. Television is not good that night, and it takes some extra scotch for him to forget his aloneness. In the haze that the scotch produces he phones someone he knows from work. His colleague says, "Charlie. I think you're on the bottle again . . . Sure, I'm your friend. But you better get some sleep so you'll be bushy-tailed in the morning. We have that big account to work on. Yeah . . . yeah . . . We can talk about that over a martini at lunch, after Mr. Big from the Agency leaves. Charlie, I just can't visit more . . . No, I just can't. See, I have some friends over and . . . (click)."

So Charlie of the high-rise spends his middle years developing alcoholism, hypertension, endocrine disturbance, ulcers, and other specifically Christian diseases. These ailments act efficiently to remove many victims of a civilization that makes little room for having friends and being friends. Isolation killed Charlie, just as it killed the old lady, both of them friendless in their different kinds of apartments. It didn't take a machine gun. All it took was "no friends."

We have friends, or we are friends, in order that we do not get killed.

Most people have forgotten the animal bands and the stories of grandfather, the survivor of the trenches. Most people know or are close to the cities with their high-rise buildings. They know, but they

cannot be friends of, the poor old lady and the rich middle-aged man. They—we—locate our lives somewhere between the extremes. Some feel absolutely friendless all the time. Most have dry stretches of life in which they have few friends and are not aware of being friends. And almost all people have had moments of barrenness or terror when the friends they counted on failed them. Wherever you are in that range of company, your memory or your imagination make it easy for you to see how we have friends, or we are friends, in order that we do not get killed.

There is dying, and there is dying. Bullets kill men in the trenches, malnutrition the friendless poor, alcohol and pills the friendless rich. But you do not need to end biological life in order to know what being killed means.

Something in you died already if you learned when you were a child that your parents were never your friends. You did not expect them to be friends alone. Sometimes they had to be authorities, and you knew it—though some parents could set the terms of order without ruling out friendliness. In fact, your parents would be anything *but* your friends if they acted like pals all the time, sloppily giving in to your every demand. But at times, at least, they should have shown that they were your friends. In the case of most of us, this they did. But your parents were only human and so were you. So there were times when they turned their backs on you. Looking back, you can admit that sometimes you deserved their shrug. At other times they simply ignored your needs. And there were times when they were closed in on themselves and left no openings for you. Maybe they were fighting each other, or worrying about your future and theirs. Maybe they were just having a good time, accidentally teaching you that you were going to have to be a friend to others outside the family circle.

Robert Louis Stevenson, I believe it was, once wrote of the moment he first felt friendless. He was four or five years old and, like all the very young, he thought until then that his parents existed only for him. When he cried, they responded. When he laughed, they thought it was funny. When he cooed, they called in the neighbors and boasted. When he was hungry, they fed him. Mother, especially, befriended him. They made up his universe until one summer evening when, as usual, he was sent to bed while it was still quite light. In the dusk Robert did not fall asleep at once. After he tired of stirring in bed he walked over to the window and looked out. On the lawn he saw his parents and their friends playing croquet in the shadows. They were teasing and chatting, goading and laughing. Yes, laughing. His mother was enjoying herself as if she did not have a care in the world. She was not thinking, for the moment, about little Robert. It was as if she did not know he existed. In her enjoyment, she did not seem to care for him.

Her chatter and her laughter were most useful, because a necessary thing had now happened to her son. He had just gotten an informing shock, a glimpse of a universe which momentarily threatened his basic trust. All the world did not organize itself around one boy, his ego, his demands and desires. If he wanted to keep his trust, he had to become aware of how gossamer was its web. Stevenson had to work with its frail threads and do some weaving of his own. The little boy dared not use that evening's discovery to work out a whole view of the world. He had added only one more element to its pieces and bits when he learned that he could not and should not always count on mother for everything. Perhaps the child's dreams that night were full of fears, but in the days and years ahead he came to know that he had to fill his life with other securities.

For another child, it may be the Fourth of July that bred this first insecurity. All the other kids were meeting next door to head for the beach and a picnic. You picture yourself in the scene. Ordinarily you would have been with the others, but something happened on the third of July to rule you out. Or maybe you were never with them, and they hardly ever noticed you. At any rate, the day stretched before you with desert bleakness while they got ready to splash. You would be hungry for the food and the fun while they mindlessly prepared to enjoy the sun. So you heard them off, the car doors slamming as if with the thud of casket lids over coffins. Melodramatic as it is to think of it that way now—the event was trivial and the world kept going on July fifth just as it had before—if you clean the cobwebs in your memory you can reenact something of the desolation of casual friendlessness you felt on an otherwise forgettable holiday. You would have just *died* to have been in that circle of friends on the beach. And something in you died, for that day at least, because you were not.

Forget it. There were other days that helped you recover. But not all memories are as obscurable as

that kind. You may recall a childhood in which you were or seemed to be friendless. Runty, you got chosen last when the sides were being selected by the Popular Kids. Pimply, you were sure it was your acne that made you such an ugly object that the others looked right past you. Shy, you were sure you were too out of place for anyone to let an eye fall on you, so others looked right through you. Overbearing, you worked so hard at finding friends that you frightened off anyone who gave you a bit of a chance. Let them make a move toward you and you pounced. Others were wary of being suffocated by anyone who needed them that much, and backed off. Clumsy, you were the butt of jokes. Innocent as you were, the cruel ones goaded you. "Come along!" they would say, and you did, gullibly traveling in their tracks. Then, far out in the country, at a signal, they broke and left you there. You heard their distant laughter from several directions but did not know which to follow, because you knew that with your heart in your throat the breath would come too slowly for you to catch up. You had to hoard that breath for the long walk to somewhere. You hoped that when you got there, no one would see the hurt in your eye, or the leftover tear.

Let such reminiscence of friendlessness mark a whole childhood and youth, and you stand the chance of becoming an adult who either has learned the great value of having a friend or being a friend, where the security of trust becomes a powerful treasure, *or* an adult who has found the power of becoming a friend atrophied, worked at too late. You can drive a person mad in a hurry, or you can choose the Chinese water torture method, with a drop and then another drop, falling on a brow through the months and the years.

"In a hurry": Yes, there are other ways to threaten what it is to be human and friendly. Some lives take their basic turn when one friend abandons another. I am not speaking here of couples divorcing or breaking up, of affairs ended or lovers quarreling. But friendship can touch lives almost as closely as can marriage or couples-loving. We have a human friend and that person becomes transparent, as it were, to a bigger, unseen world that seems friendly to us. We use the human figure or someone vivid and important to us and project it on the giant screen until it images the Way Things Are. If friendship is a sign of basic trust, we build on it to get part of our picture of the universe and even of God.

So we risk much on that important person. People confide in such friends. They tell them secrets that they would not otherwise know themselves; it is in disclosing oneself to another that one gains perspective. Think of yourself in such a relationship. Through shared confidences you bare your inmost self to your friend, and seem never quite able to recover your lost defenses. Where you choose to keep some bounds of privacy, your friend helps you set those bounds, and you rely on them. You take risks with them. You start going out of your way to try to understand what otherwise would be alien to you. You acquire new tastes, venture on new philosophies, make other friends through the original friend. Much depends on these enduring bonds.

A crisis can test such bonds. In the most earnest moment of your life, perhaps when you stand accused or on trial, everything depends on the witness of the friend. People turn to the friend, who can extricate you from the bad spot. His word is all it takes to determine whether the accuser will have to withdraw the charges. It comes down to the word of your friend against the word of the enemy. Silence falls. Benumbed, you wonder *why* silence falls. Certainly a friend will speak up in defense because he is a friend, or at least because of the truth. The longer the silence lasts, the more you feel your pulse and heartbeat. Your mouth is dry. Do you dare to let your eyes plead? As it dawns on you that you are threatened with betrayal, you do not know whether to cry out in panic or to threaten the friend with counter-betrayal. That issue settles itself: It is you who is on the spot, not your friend.

And when the silence breaks, the world falls in on you. Your friend makes misuse of the secrets you shared. He lies, and you cannot explain away the falsehood though you know that the friend knows it is a falsehood. In the aftermath, as you try to reconstruct your life, you puzzle over motives. Did I have it all wrong from the beginning? Dare I ever have another friend? Did my former friend find an advantage in abandoning me? Did he simply lack courage to side with the truth, or did someone buy him off? The puzzlement turns to despair. Years will pass, but the scar will remain, and you will have become more guarded, more tentative ever after.

If that former friend lives today, you can pay a visit, to ask what was in mind with the betrayal. Did such a person set out to "kill" you? To your surprise, you might find that the event passed from his memory, having never meant much to him. And you, too, are alive; scars, after all, are signs of a form of healing. But something in you died back then. You learned you had to believe in new life, in something to replace the old growth. You needed to relearn what it was to have a friend if you wanted to continue to be a friend. Unless you really wanted to be killed.

We have friends, or we are friends, in order that we do not get killed.

This is a book about what it means to survive—to have a friend and to be a friend.

2

An Author As a Friend

You do not become a friend by writing or reading a book but by coming into a relation with someone else. Books can keep people from such relations. You can become too engrossed in them and come to live in a self-enclosed world. In the next apartment someone may need you, but you will never know it. Books are not usually villains the way television can be, but they can preoccupy people who ought also to reach out to potential friends.

Just as a nose in a book can hide opportunities for being friends, a head full of books is not necessarily an instrument for improving friendship. The Danish thinker Soren Kierkegaard reminded us that you do not learn to swim while being suspended from the ceiling by a belt and thrashing around in the air with an instruction manual in hand. If you ever learned to ride a bicycle, it was not by reading the manual. That booklet could tell you how to put a bicycle together or take it apart. From it you could learn how to keep it in repair, or how to insure it. The manual included some rules of safety and helped you improve your cycling by telling you how to develop lung power and leg power, what kind of clothes to wear when riding, and how to make yourself small against the wind.

You learned to ride, however, because someone gave you a bicycle and urged you to get on it. Maybe a parent or a friend steadied the vehicle as you tried to get up enough courage and speed to keep it balanced. Then your instructor had to fall behind because you had to go faster than he or she could run. The first few times you had some embarrassing and painful crashes, just as the first times you swam you gulped plenty of water and had reasons to fear drowning. But you put on Band-Aids, pushed your hair back, somehow put together your pride with your eagerness, and pushed off again. After you wobbled your way safely in a parking lot, that parent or friend had to go indoors while you became more bold and experimental on the street. Your speed grew more impressive, and so did your crashes, but gradually the accidents became few and your grace as a rider grew great.

So it is with friendship. Someone can set you up for it and maybe give you a few pushes. At first there have to be steadying hands. Someone else, including an author of a book, can see some things that you are doing wrong, things you cannot see. Such a guide gains perspective from having observed many friends or having compared what others have said about friendship. Push a little harder, this author may say; hold back, you are working too hard. Be careful of obstacles! Keep your eyes wide open!

But just as the swimming teacher has to let you thrash and the bicycle tutor must let you crash, the author has to get out of the way at some point and let you deal with other people with no guidebook in hand. You may come back later with some bruises and look up a chapter or two, but a book is never a substitute for dealing with people. Of course, I do hope that this notion of the disappearing author is not so convincing that you give this book no chance!

For all that friendship means in life, we know too little about it. Social scientists and psychologists have begun to study its modern setting, but so far their findings are rather meager. And theirs is not the only kind of knowledge available or necessary. To read the statistics of marital break-ups may be a useful way of alerting us to problems between couples, but they do not address the heart.

There is a language of the heart, born of countless friendships in many ages. Some of it is religious, though the faith most of us know has surprisingly little to say about friendship. Most of its writers hurry past any talk about being friends in order to deal with what sound to them like bigger topics, including hatred and love. Yet as they hasten on, they drop important clues from their travel bags for us to pick up. We can string these together and get a fairly coherent road map for our journey into the meaning of friendship.

At the beginning of our journey, then, I am going to ask you to think of me not only as an author but also as a potential friend. Readers and writers need never meet each other except in imagination, though in the present case I might say, "Drop by, if you're passing through," or I might accept if you say, "Let's have a

cup of tea after your talk while you're in my town."
Yet even without meeting, our imaginations can
serve us well. What poses shall we assume? Should I
come on as a hardened veteran, an "old pro" in the
school of friendship? I have read some books whose
authors order the reader around in the language of
the tough and wise expert. It happens, however, that
at the end of life none of us are likely to look back
feeling that we have been fully the kinds of friends
we wanted to be. That means none of us will have the
credentials to speak too confidently. We stumble
together.

Of course, you can choose to be rather neutral
about our travel along this way as you read. I have
never felt a need to suspend my sense of distance
from an author of a manual on auto repair. Readers
and writers are not necessarily better off if they come
to feel friendly about each other while they deal with
a manual of arms in the military. But in the present
case, some conception of intimacy across the miles
and, perhaps someday, across the years will help.

You will do me a favor by being open to a friendly
reading, because I need to gain some confidence. All
my training as a professor teaches me to keep the
word *I* out of books, though it has already appeared
several times in this one. Scholars, especially historians, tend to keep themselves at a distance as they
write about people in ancient Rome, medieval
France, or modern Thailand. The reader has enough
trouble keeping track of names, dates, and places
without having to become entangled with an author
who insists on being pushed up front. What is more,
in an 850-page textbook, the string of *I*s would
become wearying: Do authors need such big ego

trips? Cannot their facts speak for themselves without help from their personalities?

If I have trouble with *I*, you may be a bit startled to find *you* so frequently on these pages. In the university they teach us to say "the reader," not *you*, to talk in the third person and not to the second person. Most books do very well without *you* in them. The owner's manual can just order you around: "1. Put the key in the ignition. 2. Now tap the accelerator pedal twice. 3. Turn the key." It works—or does it work?— the same whether or not the directions are personal. The problem is that in matters of friendship such language is not compelling. My hope for this book is that you will come to say, now and then, "Hmmm! I never thought of it that way before." And that response will come to mind more likely if "the reader" and "the writer" become you and I.

Let me forget, then, for a moment, that someone in the American Academy of Arts and Sciences might wonder what one of its members is doing speaking so far outside his specialty. I'll remember that few historians have made friendship their specialty, but that someone has to take a few timid steps along the road into the meaning of friendship. And you can forget, for a moment, that it is easier to wriggle away from an impersonal book than from a personal one, and that more challenge may come from our direct facing of each other.

Having established our tone does not solve all the problems that you may have as you think through what it means to have someone at your side on this walk. A moment ago I mentioned specialties. You may think that the sociologist who computes how many people are friends, or whether women find friendship easier than men, is a qualified expert. The psychologist or psychoanalyst, who knows much about the need for humans to surround themselves with other people, qualifies as well. The professional counselor sees hundreds of patients a year, and from such dealings gains their confidence because she can compare the ways different people mess up their friendships and thus their lives.

"The present writer" who stands behind the I of this book is none of these. He is an historian, a specialist on religion in America. He has read much biography, and become convinced that the quality of friendships or the absence of them tells more about the lives of great people than most other features. As a scholar, he is also reasonably well-read in philosophy and theology, the language about the search for meaning in life. And he will repeatedly remind you of the religious dimensions in his discussions on friendship.

Disappointed though I am by the fact that not many of the major thinkers have given long-term attention to the subject, I have been content to trail along behind those who have said something about friendship. There is no point in strewing my own trail with footnotes and other signs of academic reference. If my footnotes had footnotes and I dropped authors' names on every page in order to convince you that I am well-read or that these dropped names could substitute for my own thinking, we would lose each other along the way.

A word is in order about how and why this book came into being at all. Ordinarily I would put it up front under "Preface" or "Foreword," on those pages that few people ever read. But in a personal book it makes more sense to wait until we have each other's attention, because the beginnings tell much about the reasons. It all began with a column which, reprinted here, can serve as a start. It dates from May 30, 1979, and appeared in a magazine that saves its last page for my columns each week. Usually these columns are light-hearted, but that May I had a heavier heart. It would have been overwhelmed were it not for friends. And so the column went:

With a Little Help . . .

"In *The Valley of the Shadow* Lutheran Bishop Hanns Lilje told of his helplessness in a Nazi prison. Thirty years ago it seemed puzzling to me that he put on his agenda for future theological work an apparently banal theme. He wrote that on his last night in prison, in the face of 'the fear of death, I was able to sleep, and I see that one day I shall have to write a theological article upon sleep as one of the ways of praising God!' As the years have passed, his theme has come to seem ever more profound.

"I reread Lilje this month during my friend (and wife) Elsa's two hospital bouts with helplessness. She had lost both her parents when she was young, and was somewhat familiar with valleys and shadows. Not since the night my father almost died 40 years ago could I remember a crisis so deep. But we were by now both unpracticed at reflection, and we have talked often recently about emergent themes. Our preoccupying one also sounds banal: friendship. 'I see that one day I shall have to write a theological article upon friendship . . .' Theologians like to bite into love, power, and justice, while friendship seems bland.

34

"We take friends for granted in daily life, but when daily life disintegrates, their sustenance guards and guides our very being. Thus intercessory prayer sets in motion the tangibilification of friendship. Hand-written heartfelt greetings second the motion. Elsa's 'sisters,' people who had undergone radical mastectomies in years past, now became instant friends, though she knew few of them until this month. People from Ascension and Grace and Holy Spirit and Christ the Servant congregations leaped to life from the pages of church bulletins. Members of one of these congregations, for example, visited us with a full dinner the first several nights Elsa was home. Were we special? 'No, they did it for all their members and friends. . . .'

"We did have access to one elite that seemed to play favorites. Our bishop phoned often, and seven clerically collared friends visited regularly. One hospital roommate pondered what particularly heinous sins Elsa had committed that she needed so much help. A week later another thought that Elsa must be dying. Why else would 'reverends' keep coming? Here again, 'They do it for all their members and friends,' and for some enemies too.

"Those collars aside, we were in no way exceptional. Proof of that came as we observed the network of friendships in the 'ethnic' hospital. Let the sociobiologists tell us that generosity and altruism are nothing but expressions of the relentlessly selfish gene. They are wrong. Let cynics say that friendship represents the selfish 'like seeking like,' people acting prudentially for the day when they need help. They, too, are wrong.

"Back in my pastoral years I resolved to have nothing to do with theologies that have nothing to say to people waiting for verdicts in surgical waiting rooms. Now I add a new resolve: to have nothing to do with 'go it alone' religiosities that do not even seek congregating and community. And I shall continue to puzzle over the paucity of comment about friendship in the theological dictionaries and libraries. Most of all, having again been befriended, we shall seek to be friends, to try harder to locate the friendless, who remain the world's majority."

The weeks passed, and my wife and I headed for an island where we summer, this year for her to recuperate. Along came a letter from the publisher who was puzzled that, while I was puzzled over the absence of books on friendship, I had made no move to venture one myself. I have other writing projects; this one had never occurred to me. But, he wrote, you must have thoughts on the subject. Of course I did, and was getting more every day. Without suspending those other projects, I began to gather notes, readings, and books during the months when Elsa and I took pains as a couple to sit back a little more, to be together more thoughtfully. You will understand this chapter better if I quote a memo I later sent to my editor:

"One problem with me as an author: It is part of my personality and vocation as a professor, writer of serious books, and columnist, to be a bit diffident about self-revelation, and a book on friendship demands self-revelation. I am not shy—anything but that—but I tend to write about a person with my initials who sits a foot and a half away from me. I showed you a new book I wrote for a series on 'faith journeys.' The publisher wanted the authors to reveal themselves on the journey. My brother read the book and said that he enjoyed it as an exercise not in self-revelation but in self-concealment. 'It's as if you are saving yourself in case some day you are to write a real autobiography.' You know you will have to prod me to overcome this problem."

Prodded I have been. But you will excuse me if most of the time I point beyond my autobiography to people who have led their lives on a scale that terrifies or delights me. We can learn more from them. And you will pardon me, I hope, if more often than not I throw the issue of friendship on a screen that has room for images drawn from a longer history than that of my fifty plus years. No one life can capture enough of what we need to reflect about. I can only say that whatever is here is fused through and worked through my own experience.

What else do you need to know about the author as a potential friend? That he has had more friends than he deserves. That he puts a high premium on the part they play in an otherwise too busy and too pre-occupied life. That he welcomes the interruptions they provide, the way they can with a phone call disrupt a schedule in order to make days turn out better than they should have. That he has a wife and a family made up of friends more friendly than the manuals say one should expect them to be. That he has a lot to learn, and that this book represents a stage along the way. That he wishes life were long enough that we would not be ships passing on a summer's night and that we could all get to know each other. And that he still has a problem getting to know you through the instrument of this book and a library full of books. Let's face that systematically.

I am not a psychologist whose practice in clinics will inform our conversing about being friends. My way of life does not leave occasions for me to hang out in neighborhood bars or other places where I can come up with do-it-yourself kits for common-sense approaches to being friends. My world surrounds me with books. Our home has little room for pictures, because almost all the walls are crowded with bookshelves and thus with books. My work takes me to a library with millions of volumes. So for our conversing I would like to think that the books can be of much help.

Books have limits, however. We do not become human beings because we think. One of my books, by a friend I have met only on pages, Eugen Rosenstock-Huessy, makes the case that we are humans more because we are befriended or beloved than because we think. As children of God we are brought into being by a call, "Who art thou . . . that I should care for thee?" As babies, before our thinking helps us, we are survivors because of the care of older people. All through our lives we stutter and stammer as we try to answer the call, "Who art thou . . . ?" and the sign that we are cared for. Herein lies our humanity. We sort out the offers made to us in a world full of temptations. "We wish to follow the deepest question, the central call which goes straight to the heart, and promises our soul the lasting certainty of being inscribed in the book of life."

In the same book, Rosenstock-Huessy points to the limits of what books can tell us. "The presence of one living soul among the three million volumes of a great library offers sufficient proof against the notion that the secret of this soul is to be found by reading those three million books." But though we are people whose existence is based more in our response to a call or to love and friendship than in thinking, this does not mean that thinking and the wisdom of books have nothing to do with our existing. We read books to learn *about* what being a friend has meant, what having a friend can mean. We have to take that "about" kind of knowledge into ourselves and then engage each other as persons, as if we are working past the page on which this appears in order to get to each other. This is not just a book about an idea called friendship, which is an abstract notion, but about being a friend, which is a reality full of flesh and blood and life.

That idea came from one of the "three million" library books, so Rosenstock-Huessy would not have scorned us as we add one more, to make the total three million and one. In the library I consult my shelves and the library cards. My fingers run down the tables of contents and indices at the back of books. Certainly talk about what *friend* means must fill hundreds of thousands of the pages in thousands of the volumes. It must, that is, if the books want to do justice to the space friendship plays in the lives of most whole and healthy humans.

Unless I am missing something, however, I am *really* missing something. The books and paragraphs on friendship are surprisingly sparse, except for some recent ones grounded in psychology. Take a moment to browse in my personal library with me, and especially in its reference section, which is our best bet.

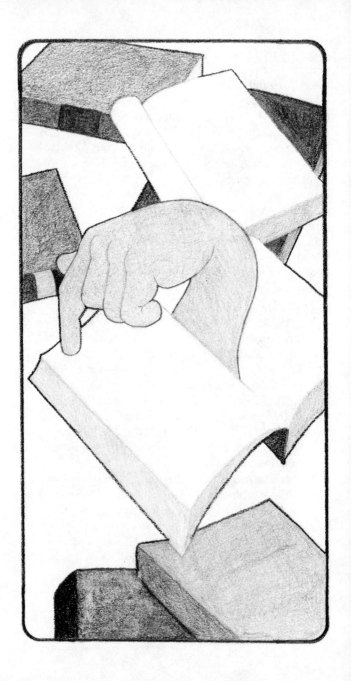

Philosophy. The philosophers inquire about the meaning of words, sentences, and of life itself. The world is fired at us point-blank, says one. The world is present to us, so we are "condemned to meaning," says another. So we expect philosophers to concentrate on something as meaning-full as a friend. The eight volumes of a superb *Encyclopedia of Philosophy* contain 8,412 columns. Between "Freud, Sigmund" and "Fries, Jakob" there is no space for "Friendship." In Volume Five I follow up the one index reference to "Friends of God," a mystical group from the fourteenth century. The Friends of God get ten lines, but except for the accident of their marvelous name they do not inform our quest.

On the soil of my own university and then in offices of an encyclopedia nearby, philosophers tried to clump learning into a "syntopicon"—don't look for that invention in your dictionary—of *The Great Ideas*. Friendship did not make it among the 102 great ones. The editors kindly include an "inventory of terms" at the end, and "Friendship" is there. According to this index, if we want to learn about friendship we must "*See* LOVE." Love is big among the Great Ideas, while posed against it friendship seems undramatic. But the indexers do us a favor by pointing to the traces of concern for friendship among the philosophers. The big names are there: Sophocles has a mention, Plato shows a concern, and Aristotle receives a trophy for paying most attention. Then come a couple of Christians, Augustine who deserves notice, and Aquinas, the giant so far as this topic is concerned. Among the moderns, the Great Books and Great Ideas people can point to names like Montaigne and Kant, Tolstoy and Freud.

FRIEDRICH, JOHANNES
German Church historian. He
First *Vatican Council, opposed
of Papal [Infallability and, refusing
decrees of the Council, he
municated in 1871. He was a
member of the *Old Catholic
later withdrew.

friendship !!!

nglish
to
other-
reorga-
oses; it
stone-
atin coun-
le to the
ny, and the
an undoc-
been
Church

g attributed to
e text of Mk. 16:
x 'W', now in the

In the Hebrew
he three forms of
–16), so named
hat legal demands
s the term has been
hruch finance.

FRITH, JOHN (c. 150
martyr. In 1525 T. *Wolsey
canon in 'Cardinal College
Oxford. He was imprisone
but escaped to Marburg,
*Tyndale. On his return i
and condemned to de
*purgatory and *tra
necessary dogmas.

FROBEN, JOHN (c.
scholar. In 1491 he sta
worked in conjunctio
from c. 1513 with D
printed the first editi
and several of the

COMMUNION. See
of.

UARD (1863-1938), Bp.
High Church-

FROISSART, JEA
From

But there is mainly sagebrush on our desert. All of them have to slight friendship when they come up against love.

Try the encyclopedia. The editors of *The Encyclopaedia Britannica* include an article on the religious group "The Friends," who have some things to teach us, but these are not exactly to the point of our topic. And in the encyclopedia's catalog of many thousands of items we find in three lines that Ralph Waldo Emerson wrote an essay on the topic and in four lines more each that there are spaceships and an airport in Baltimore called Friendship.

Religion matches philosophy for dealing with the deep topics, and claims to reach even further to the unseen, the ultimate, and God. In the Western world, we begin this topic biblically. *The Interpreter's Dictionary of the Bible* matches *The Encyclopedia of Philosophy* for quality and almost in bulk, with its 7,696 columns. Only part of one of them deals with "Friend, Friendship," and "Friend of the King." I did not know until I read the second of these that Abimelech had a formal friend named Ahuzzath, and that Zabad and Husai also held that office.

In 1976, fourteen years after their original work, the *Interpreter's Dictionary*'s editors came out with a supplement of 1,974 more columns, not quite two of which deal with "Friend, Friendship in the New Testament." Things are looking up, because in those years there was a gain in space from .0001299 of the whole to .0011148. Don't fault those editors for slighting the term. The *Complete Concordance* to the Bible, a book that alphabetizes the uses of all but a few words (like "a" and "the") in a modern version includes 4,315 columns, about two of which deal with our "friendly" terms. That means that about .0004636 of the important words in the English Bible are *friendship* or *friend*. Needless to say, *love* is far more frequent and, in its way, more important.

Theologians and scholars of religion reflect on words in the various scriptures. For formidable learning we turn to bearded and scowling Germans, who left a seven-volume monument called *Die Religion in Geschichte und Gegenwart* [religion in history and the present]. The Germans ran over all the religions with vacuum-cleaner efficiency and thoroughness, and found only enough comment for half a column on friendship in world religions and three good columns on the same theme in ethics. You could easily thumb right past them.

As a Christian I look for Christian comment on the theme, and turn to a typical encyclopedia. *Sacramentum Mundi* comes in six-volume magnificence from German Catholic circles, and these six volumes manage to overlook "Friendship" entirely.

Clearly, pushed up into competition with "Love," "Friendship" seems a bit safe and domestic, nice to have around, but drab enough to blend in with the wallpaper. The titans take on "Love" and leave "Friendship" to mere mortals. We have to pay close attention to those rare pages in the library where "Friendship" gets its due. Among living souls like the one who reads among three million books or who browses with me in my library, being friends is an urgent theme. We must begin at the beginning.

3

Becoming Friends: An Act of Freedom

You will cherish friends most if you think of your relation to them as an act of creation and an act of freedom. Compare friendship to the creation of the universe. In the biblical picture, it did not *have* to be. Page one simply says, "In the beginning God created the heavens and the earth." And "then God said, 'Let us make man in our image, after our likeness. . . .'" So with any friendship with a particular person. It did not have to be. Both of you were on your own courses, unaware that the other existed. You met your payrolls or punched the time clocks without thinking of another. You turned your papers in on time and got back the grades on report card day, with nothing on your mind except studies.

Then, somehow one day you bumped into each other. It looked like an accident that you were next in line at the cafeteria. You met her at a concert on a night when you almost did not go, but how could you have missed Dietrich Fischer-Dieskau? Or you were moving into that third floor apartment, and your legs had given out. How nice that someone came along from the fourth floor to help lug the sofa. The fourth of your foursome did not show up for tennis, but that lanky fellow who practices his serve in the far court each Monday was available.

You can forget 999 out of 1,000 people you bump into in cafeteria lines, at concerts, in apartment hallways, or on tennis courts. There is no reason to become involved. Life's choices include the choice *not* to make friends, or not to relate to particular people. To make too many friends is to debase the coinage of friendship, since you could not devote yourself to the art if you defined it too broadly and spread yourself too thin. In making a friend, you had the freedom to act—and you did.

Freedom, in most people's minds and books, is far from friendship. Friendship is for fun, and freedom is for fighters. The Jesuit Walter Ong mourns our tendency to ignore the link between freedom and play. "Freedom is grim—something to be fought for, something that we feel may confront us with antagonisms and even hatred instead of generating effusiveness and spontaneity and joy." Yet God acted in spontaneity and joy in creating the world as an act of divine freedom. One of the Psalms even has him making the sea monster Leviathan as an act of playful freedom, "for the sport of it." So you create friendship, by letting it happen when you locate certain qualities in another person. With good humor you pursue these qualities and come close to that person, fully aware that you do not have to. You are

embarking on a course that, as we will see, drives dictators mad and confuses those who want to program your life.

The chemistry of friendship, at least at the point of its birth, is a mystery. This mystery is not like that of the detective story, on whose last page everything is revealed. The mysteries that matter remain veiled even after many outer veils disappear. We do not exhaust the secrets they shroud. So the analysts of friendship can never quite explain why any two persons are friends. "What does he find in that person? They seem so different!"

But friendship does not usually occur between mere opposites. The friend seeks some basis for communion. For instance, many of my friends are historians and professors. You may find them a dull lot, because they spend a lot of time in cobwebbed attics or the dust of libraries. I find them exciting, since together we ask questions about what it is to be human and, through our stories, try to help other people imagine what it would have been like to be someone else, somewhere else. We take delight in our work just as artists or athletes do, but we may also believe that it may inform the human story. When society stops to think, it may have to reflect upon what we have learned and seen. We will not look as interesting as sky divers or rock stars. But we do have a kind of communion.

My world would be poorer if it had only professors in it. We could refine our craft and forget the rest of life. So, like most of them and most of you—look around you—I cherish friendships with people whose daily work I do not begin to understand. They are insurance salespersons, accountants, coaches. We courteously ask each other how the work is going, but thirty seconds of reply settles that. Then we talk about what brings us together: old memories. The experience of having lived near each other. The way we brought up our children. Where we are vacationing. The concert. The wine. Politics.

What makes my spirit come alive to such persons and not to others? Why do so many who share my profession have nothing but professional relations? Why are we content to let them be that way? My friends and I do not merely converge on common interests, though I am more likely than not to hang out with people of my politics, my faith, my hobbies, my tastes. Do I think that my friends are better than other people? No, the human race had *better* have better examples and models than my seedy crowd and I. Most of us could list members of the opposite sex more attractive-looking than the person who is our spouse, but we are not interested in being married to these others. In each other we saw something that gave rise to communion, and we consider each other irreplaceable. Some instinct seems to be in operation. We divine that this other person is worth taking the risks for; will he, will she be open to these risks from the other side?

There is no reason to make the search for friendship sound like an animal instinct. Friendship does not always come as the result of a search; it can come when we least look for it, just as it denies itself when we pursue it too earnestly and with pathetic eagerness. In some sense the friend simply confronts us as the stranger who need not, must not, remain a stranger. But we have become open to friendship because in the course of our growing up we also developed certain values. By values, I do not mean objects of value, like "brown shoes." I mean consistent tilts toward something, like "preferring brown shoes." Through the years I have found that black patents looked too formal, and track shoes too informal. For my costumes, thinks a particular woman, brown shoes work best. And she meets someone else who does not necessarily prefer brown shoes, but who has developed means for deciding what clothes suit her best. They have a prior chance for communion because of "clothes-tasteness." When they overcome the initial strangeness, there is something for them to talk about and compare. Of course, not all people who have thought through apparel preferences will automatically become friends. They can walk right past the sales clerk or the garment worker, and not give the time of day to fashion designers. Meanwhile the very ordinary woman in the next office, an amateur in the subject of shoes and clothes, is emotionally available to give a personal stamp to the desire for communion. Unless she "answers back," friendship cannot begin. Pestering someone for opinions is not a sign of friendship. Both sides have to *will* the relation, or it will languish and die soon after birth.

Sometimes friendship just falls on unsuspecting people. A searcher comes to a group, perhaps a church or a club, a chapter of Alcoholics Anonymous or a political caucus. This searcher is after a thing, not a person: a belief or a hobby, a cure or a cause. Along the way, he makes a friend. Such friendship is orthodox and relies on communion of the like-minded. But there is another kind based on choice. Peter Berger reminds us that the Greek word for

choice was *haeresis,* which stands behind the word heresy, the opposite of orthodoxy. The herd lets itself be pushed together in the same corral, while the heretic strays. The mass of people resent the stray, because he represents a freedom they find denied them, or a threat to their herd instinct.

Friends do well to cross the boundaries of natural habit and to move into the realm of choice, at least part of the time. For instance, many people establish casual friendships with those who "live next door." Because of the accident of a common wall or fence, they have to make do with each other's presence. Often, these ways of being a friend are an additional luxury in life, a bonus or a plus added to all other relations. At least Jones and a neighbor are not taking each other to court over the boundary, or hassling each other's children whenever a ball goes over the property line. At best this means sharing an occasional can of beer or birthday cake with that friend next door.

Others parlay that easy friendship into the only kind they have and build all their alliances, including the most intimate, with the people who are immediately available. That usually means people of the same income group—since American housing patterns tend to follow social class lines—and with people who in many other ways represent little difference.

Heretical friendship enriches life by crossing such boundaries. Race, for one. Having a friend who is white provides access to a thought world denied many members of the black minority. Without such a friend, they may see the majority as nothing but oppressors instead of as individuals who are often weak and frightened themselves. Vice versa, the black friend shatters stereotypes and opens a world of wonderful variety to members of a white majority. In many northern cities, mobile people will often—and I invite you to test this in your own circle to see if I should not be saying "will ordinarily"—have not a single reasonably close friend of another race, even though they may work with them, play racquetball with them, send their children to school with them, and do business with them. Banter across a bar or an office desk does not constitute friendship. Friendship involves a more sustained kind of opening.

If the future of the world is to be as full of fanaticism and intolerance as it bids fair to be, the prophecy of historian Hugh Thomas could come true. In the next century, he writes, the great human divisions may follow religious lines, not national lines. Religious zealotry is particularly prone to extreme suspicion of the non-orthodox, and because of this it poses special dangers to champions of variety and reform. The 1980s have seen a promise of Thomas's prediction in the new fanaticisms of all religions: in Shi'ite Islam in Iran, among the Gush Emunim of Israel, the Soka Gakkai in Japan, and the new Fundamentalists of the United States. People are gathering into tribes, into separatenesses that can help them keep their place and ward off the presumed or real threats of outsiders.

In times like these, tolerance becomes too weak an attitude to be of help. Being tolerant has come to mean being wishy-washy, having no deep commitments. Because of its shallowness, tolerance has gotten a bad name and picked up some enemies who like to play into the hands of the intolerant. Only those who are certain are truly religious, they say. Only fundamentalism and fanaticism count for faith in such a market. Fanaticism, however, can exact terrible penalties in a world too full of weaponry, too ready for terrorism, too tiptoed toward the brink of religio-racial-cultural-ethnic warfare on almost all continents.

As religious communities feel threatened today, there is some understandable backing off from religiously mixed marriages. After decades of openness to other communities, Reform Judaism in the 1970s suddenly revealed a somewhat closed-off face. Rabbis were to be forbidden participation in mixed marriages between Jews and Christians or others. How standoffish, some thought. Yet the rabbis pointed out that with Israel jeopardized, Jewish identity insecure, many Jews not practicing, Jewish families declining in size, and, finally, with many children of Jewish-Gentile marriages departing from Judaism, mixed marriage had become too high a risk. Judaism could not survive another two generations of such loss.

Other faiths have also stepped back from intermarriage, despite or because of the erosive climate of the day. Until the Second Vatican Council (1962-65) few Protestants were close friends of their Catholic neighbors. They might vote together, politic together, and work together, but leisure habits and friendship patterns they developed apart. Then when the churches grew more friendly, so did their members. With the bars down, mixed marriages became a threat to both communities. A new defensiveness has started to threaten the steps to Christian unity.

Whether among the religions of all continents, or in North America between Christians and Jews or Protestants and Catholics, "heretical" friendships, worked at because they are chosen, now provide the best basis for mutual understanding between groups. Probably nothing would better serve to set back the menace of fanaticism and intolerance than a massive breakthrough of intergroup friendships.

People of commitment have learned to understand other people of differing commitments, thanks to friendships forged by foreign student programs or travel. To be befriended in a land where few speak one's language is often the beginning of a lifelong bridge-building activity. American families who have exposed their children and their children's high schools to visiting students have often made possible heretical friendships. These call upon the hosts not to desert their own beliefs and ties, but to guarantee to others the security they insist on with their own.

Most of us can test the value of the exceptional "not next door" friendship by recalling the most timid versions of these in our own lives. We take the infant steps first to gain confidence. In my recall now, I come far down from the drama of relating Muslims and Jews and Christians to recount the beginnings of a friendship with one of my own kind, a friendship that came at a crucial moment in my life and has enhanced the days and years that followed immeasurably.

At mid-century many of us who were preparing for the ministry at a seminary came from a rigid set of feeder prep schools. From an eighth of an inch away these schools all looked alike, but to their denizens, they were truly tribalist. Confuse a Lithuanian with a Latvian or an Estonian by calling them all Baltic, and you have some sense of distance between these look-alikes. At seminary the prep school friendship patterns remained frozen, affecting students' choices of dormitory and roommates, colleagues and fellow club-members, and even curricular and vocational decisions. Being of the herd, I automatically shared the pattern of orthodox friendships.

Then, near the end of our first year, a violator of the clubby lines came to see me after class one day. He seemed a bit stiff and formal, possibly slightly uneasy. He was doing what was not done in a world of high conformity. I did not know him well, except to recognize our differences. He was a semi-professional pitcher while I could not catch a nerf ball if it was handed to me. My conversation partner toured with a singing choir while they confined me to the nether shower stalls. I savored the typewriter and no one yet foresaw his writing talent, now polished through five books. He had a prominent nose and I a daily more prominent brow. I dwell on these apparent trivia only to stress the distances that exist even in the world of the "likes."

"Marty, have you a roommate yet for next year?"

"Probably. I suppose I'll do as I've been doing."

"Why don't you encourage X to room with someone from St. John's College?"

"Where does that leave me?"

"With someone else from St. John's College. Me. How about it?"

He went on to give a little review of inbreeding and its hazards. Three or four years after prep schools and colleges, the old school ties were still knotting seminarians, or shortening their horizons. We should break the pattern. Whoever knows the history of Old School Ties in England, the tangles of Ivy in New England, the closedness of Greek letter societies, or the network of Ole Boys in Georgia has some clue to the power of male bonding on orthodox and introverted lines. My new friend and I rehearsed the history of such ties and began a reflection that has led both of us to be uncommonly devoted to friendship as a theological theme and, I would like to think, to its expression, which has been enriched in the subsequent three decades.

A trivial tale this is. But whoever digs up counterparts to such slight overcomings in his own life can also point to ways in which these led to ever bolder heretical steps in the choice of friends. Heresy in its own generation seems dangerous. It is, since it calls into question what the secure want to keep secure. But a generation later we often honor the heretic for some of the proceeds that came from choice.

When people think about the values of friendship, it is not likely that many of them will worry about how it connects with public order. In fact, they may not think much about public order at all. But there are good reasons for concern about the possible disintegration of friendly interpersonal relations in a world that leans increasingly toward mass-managed or totalitarian ways of life. We have already seen the impact of unorthodox friendships on barriers of intolerance. How does this power of choice translate to the political arena?

It is efficient for governments to run lives as if there are no exceptions and varieties. Line up the herd and you can better direct it. Allow it no withholding of consent and you can drive it where you wish. Most people in the world live under repressive regimes of right and left which set out to kill variety. One line of propaganda over one broadcast band determines what news the people shall hear and what styles of living they must follow. The enforcers of the rules listen carefully. Surveillance is everywhere—or is feared to be everywhere, which amounts to the same thing. People are to engage in groupthink, the group being always as big as the nation, and the thought being only that of the regime.

Such total control may not be an immediate threat in North American society, in part because of a tradition of freedom and in part because of the variety of people that grace the shores and land. Some prophets look ahead, however, and picture the possibility of a great new depression, after which people might wish to reorganize the whole economy. Or it might happen that as terrorism grows, they would want to give up civil liberties and demand control of popular opinion and public gatherings. In such circumstances, it is likely that the nations would have to make a god of the state, and allow for no deviations. As they used to say, it *can* happen here.

In the meantime, the best safeguard against society's becoming an idol, and an encroaching one at that, seems to lie in nurturing what Edmund Burke called "little platoons." Sociologists today give them another name, appropriate to the formidable language of social science. They are "mediating structures." Among those usually listed are neighborhoods, families, churches, and clubs. To them we now add the circles of friendship. They are so effectively subversive of the totalitarian regime because they are hardest to organize and control. Who belongs to them? Can you right now write a list of all your rather close friends and rule out everybody else? The borders of the circle are fortunately open, and people are reckless about membership lists. Who pays dues? Does anyone?

Friendship does not disappear among free spirits under dictatorship. Indeed, it is sometimes born of comradely resistance and the need for mutual survival. People nurture it because they have weathered experiences together. They come to admire each other and to hide together. As friends they dream of freedom. They know who they are, but they do not know *exactly* who they are. Yet as they dig in and set out to outlast the regime, they almost automatically offer resistance. They will not let themselves be mashed into the lockstep of being like everyone else. They learn how to keep fingers crossed, to filter signals from the regime, to teach people how to engage in creative foot-dragging, to keep their sanity. They tell the stories that produced their friendship and that result from it.

Apart from totalitarianism—or before it comes in the form of a regime that allows for no diversity or dissent—societies that still include more freedom do well to cultivate all those little platoons that make takeover difficult. Because they are a different form of mediating ideas and beliefs, they provide their members with the means to analyze and to resist. When the state meets mistrust, these networks gain in credibility. Among these platoons again we find the circle of friends, or, better, the set of overlapping circles. They do not mesh well with anyone who must have on hand a list of controllable units. Then they offer resistance or help their members outlast the regime that replaces public order with total control.

In North America the public idea is endangered by the opposite challenge, the idea of a purely private existence. Whether or not society survives seems less the concern of many than whether they can get their benefit out of what is left of it. Political candidates offer no vision; they promise to try to keep the old machinery wired together and oiled for two or four more years. Candidates for the Master of Business Administration degree try to become technically expert, but they are often less likely to think deeply about the economic order they are entering, or whether they can play a part in preserving or transforming it. Students line up to enter the professions of medicine or law without asking whether the culture and institutions which support or rely on them can survive. They are often more interested, and they admit it, only in what they can get out of the survivals. They want the goodies of the American Ways of Life, but then withdraw to the private sectors of life and hide in their high-rises or escape on the long weekends.

In the presence of such attitudes, political parties lose their legitimacy as people turn independent, which usually means uninvolved. Politics disappears. Religion becomes a private affair. As expressions of freedom, these individualisms are good balances to Big Brother. But they also leave people powerless. For that reason many counsel that individuals be connected with each other in the little platoons. Society, in these terms, is a community of sub-communities which sometimes compete, often go on parallel tracks, and on occasion interact.

Such a model of society is very much the one for which I work. But even its components can be so large that we are lost in them. Roman Catholics are 50,000,000 strong in the United States, and many parishes have thousands of members. Catholics may join groups for common action or prayer, but even these often belong to remote bureaucracies. The first zone of sociality beyond the family, then, is the bond between friends, or what we are calling the circles of friends. My friends and I can resist more readily than can any of us alone. If we together respond to a signal, we can test whether it is worth following up on. When one of us tires, the others can nudge. Most of all, the worth of the values of which we are a part needs confirming not just through print or over airwaves but by the living voice of someone we can check out, with whom we can reason.

Few political treatises talk about the role of the friend in the public order. When first he drafted the Declaration of Independence, Thomas Jefferson wanted to include the notion that a republic was built on affection. That meant that the act of crossing the ocean was already a declaration of independence, for it meant a turning of the back on old bonds. The people who came to new shores were free to be affectionate toward each other and to be friends of the soil itself. Jefferson did not foresee the crowded and impersonal society that would replace his colonies with their villages and farms. But he did have a clue that few have picked up on later. It is my hunch that the most durable public people—and this does not necessarily mean the leaders who have cronies—are those who in friendship take pains to see to it that museums remain open, symphonies and operas get a hearing, welfare agencies find volunteers. Were I a dictator, the first connections I would wish to interrupt—and the last I could successfully break—would be the networks of friends.

Behind Jefferson and modern American order there is a long heritage of thought connecting friendship to democracy on a grander scale. In ancient China Confucius did so in his *Analects*, and Cicero saw friendship as nurturing the spread of equality and thus of democratic thinking. It has been common to think of the channels of friendship as conduits of civil life, carriers of news about griefs and joys. We do not have to think on that grand a scale; these just-mentioned thinkers may have come closer to what we would now call the idea of fraternity, and not to anything as intimate or committed as the model of friendship which we see as the great humanizer of life.

Once you open the topic of friendship, however, a whole string of "and that reminds me's" comes to mind. Friendship and republicanism are models for each other in still another respect: Friendship is a sign of freedom. No one is able to force you and me to be friends. They can force us to be taxpayers, soldiers, citizens. But they cannot exact from us emotions that go with affection.

Civil life is based in part on honor, and friendship has to rely on it. We do not necessarily seek or gain advantages through being friends. Without signing contracts, however, people do "honor friendships." These relations serve as training grounds for other kinds of commitments, and thus help teach us the fidelity that has to become second nature in the public order.

Friendship has to be given; no one can take it or demand it or force it. And for this reason, some have seen in friendship a contributor to equality. I have seen Francis Bacon quoted on this notion: "A man cannot speak to his son but as a father, to his wife but as a husband, to his enemy but upon terms; whereas a friend may speak as the case requires, and not as it sorteth out with the person." Perhaps Bacon is right, but I remain suspicious because his equals all belonged to the elite. Probably a good deal of class distinction remains in such a world. The rich and poor, the powerful and powerless do not have much occasion or motivation to cross such boundaries for friendships. Still, since people are more nearly free whenever they are less controllable, having friends even within one's own class is one more way to keep from regimentation and assure an expanse of freedom in a healthy society.

So much for controlling regimes and the public order. At the opposite extreme, revolutionaries and fanatics do not have room for friendship either. People involved in a cause welcome comrades, since they need the association of others who will forget everything and die with them for the cause. With comrades they can eat the revolution, they can drink it, write poetry to it, make love to it, sing songs to it. But comrades who · together celebrate only their shared cause are not really friends. Friends do not "forget everything." They remember the costly sacrifices that make life worth living. They want their needs to be remembered. They may wish to whisper to a friend when the cause needs silence, while an enemy of the revolution waits to hear the source of sound so he can kill. A friend does not share in every detail the ideology of the cause and its supporters. The friend asks, "Are you sure?" and "Why?" and "Who are we to be so righteous?" and "Have we forgotten something?"

In the United States the public often criticizes high officials, and most notably its presidents, for the company they keep. In some cases the persons closest to the president stand furthest apart from the appointed staff. The staff has to be efficient, invisible, and cool. Bureaucracies need people who do not make waves, who can look serene as ducks gliding on water. The ducks may be paddling like hell to keep moving, with their webbed feet out of sight; the bureaucrats may face frustration or crises. An observer would never know it. But the friend is inefficient, visible, and warm. He or she might create disturbances when the cameras discover the friendship. Friends sometimes make jokes and gestures that embarrass other officials. They are not always discreet in their actions; they *think* they can "get away with something" because they *can* get away with something. Their important friend forgives them.

Though such friendships sometimes have an unsavory dimension and produce minor public scandals, overall they serve excellently to remind us that even the most important organizers of life may welcome its pleasantly unorganized portions. Presidents who deal all day with causes and caucuses, coteries and clienteles, cults and citizens, like to doff their official clothes at end of day, take off their shoes, put their feet on a hassock, and pop open a beer or sip some bourbon among a circle of friends. How inefficient of them; how human. Those hours may be the best for the republic. During them the worst cannot often happen. Because friendship resists being organized, it helps make possible the tenderly human.

Fanatics have no room for such friendship because they are overcompensating for personal doubts that the friend raises again. The fanatic has to be sure, has to be obsessively convinced that he is "doing what the Lord would do in the circumstance if the Lord were in full possession of the facts." The friend knows that the Lord has the facts and that mortals can only buzz around and spin their wheels, creating the impression that the human dominators really are in control. And because he or she is a friend, the right questions get raised at the wrong moments. All that is fortunate for the enemies of fanaticism.

A friend is strategically placed for the good of people who would otherwise be victims of dictators, presidents, and fanatics. Likewise, the absence of friends is costly for people who are rising to power. I know of a church leader who became quite an entrepreneur. While other leaders huffed and puffed in their efforts to achieve great things, only to reach limits, this gifted person charged ahead. The ventures he undertook were grandiose enough; the media had to pay attention. But as time passed, the leader seemed to lose perspective. Celebrity became more important than the church; each act had to be more sensational than the previous one. In the end, the leader's ventures came to seem exaggerated and even gross.

Critics arose. Some of them said that the leader had become such a caricature that he was distorting the faith itself. Yet as they checked his achievements against the standards to which he would have agreed, most of which came from the Bible, it was impossible to say that he was entirely out of line. His faults were the faults of exaggeration and grossness; he pushed something so far that it changed character. What had begun to serve people now served the fame of the servant. Efforts designed for the glory of God supported the glory of the leader. But it was the scale that was wrong, not all the original intentions. One day some editorial critics touched the sore point. Puzzling over the fact that a good cause had gone wrong, they concluded that what the leader lacked was friends. He had plenty of admirers and employees. But at many points along the way a friend would have asked, "Say, aren't you going too far this time?" or "Come off it, won't you?" Instead, the high achiever was on his own, friendless, able to measure life only by the new standards of success that he set himself. He seemed mild, cool, and poised, but no red-eyed fanatic was more detached from reality than he.

When you seek to develop a circle of friends, the best advice that the history of friendship can offer is this: Be sure some of you can laugh. Friends laugh together. They have laughed in political prisons even though they knew they were under sentence. When hostages find release after long confinement, they often speak of friends they found in captivity. And when they do, they testify to the ability such friends had to smuggle humor under the noses of captors. They invented games and devised subtle taunts that kept the guards off balance. Together the captive friends had taken the measure of the boundaries of life. They knew they might die or, worse, might face torture. But having done the measuring together, they could find that they had not sold their souls. They really remained in command, so they could laugh at the forces against them.

Most of us do not live with such high drama, and do not want to. But in the quieter schemes of life, we still welcome the fact that the friend helps us laugh. Coffee breaks are dangerous for bureaucracies when employees become friends and one of them cracks jokes. Tyrant schoolmasters have never known how to handle students who at recess time exercise friendship. Their smiles need not be sneering or defiant. They just show by their light-heartedness that no one can buy their souls or force them into line. Friendship fits between the cracks in life. It breaks through the little chinks where the sun was supposed to be forbidden, or seeps under locked doors. Nothing, including distance, can deny it. And it is tentacular; it reaches out and attaches itself to otherwise bare walls, or makes connections where everything was supposed to be kept apart. It sees the comedy of life where the command was to be grim.

Friendship is one of the freest forms of association in most cultures. When we marry, we have to appear before an officer of the law and sign a legally binding document. While "palimony," the financial commitment one takes on when there has been a sexually-based liaison, is yet in dubious legal territory, more and more counselors advise people to work things out contractually. To adopt a child or to take in children for foster care involves a network of agency concerns. The law has its stand in such matters. Life insurance and social security are governmentally supervised or administered. We sign contracts with firms. A credentialling agency decides whether my college is accredited and therefore whether it pays me to go there or not, since graduate schools also pay attention to the credentialling. I may have trouble getting a job, no matter how qualified I may be, if my school lacked accreditation. A state Board of Education also looks at standards. I have to be licensed to drive a bus.

No one, however, signs papers in friendships. This does not mean that there are no forms of friendly relation in which a contract is not in order. When there are large financial considerations, friends do themselves and their heirs or dependents a favor by getting it all in print. Such a contract can liberate them for other acts of friendship. But the contract has to do with the transaction, not with the formation and base of friendship itself. Society as a whole does not regulate, prevent, or encourage friendship.

Insofar as it falls into a zone apart from such external controls, friendship, like play, takes on the character of freedom. Children in Little League have already entered the adult world of programs, and one can make a case for its routines and pressures as

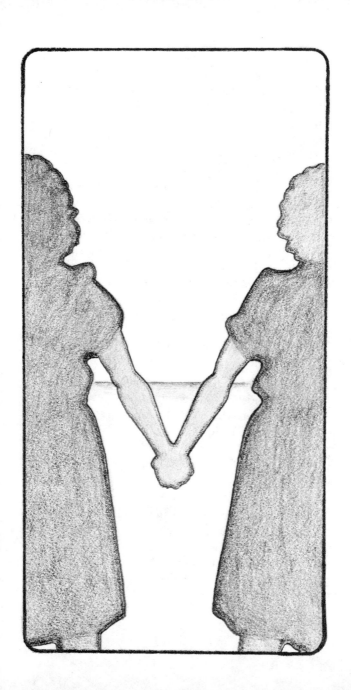

preparations for the grimmer dimensions of life. But children who play on sandlots or who picnic in the woods can improvise. If they do not like one game, they play another; if they do not enjoy one way of playing a game, they find another way. Not having good athletic equipment is no inhibition at all. They can imagine themselves inventing, as they "make do." Friendship has that character.

The employer has a line-staff flow chart and the manager a baseball line-up. Assistant professors become associate professors and sophomores need their credits in order to become juniors. Marital incompatibility or desertion can allow a spouse to break up the contract of a marriage, whether the partner desires it or not. "Lots of luck: I'm leaving." But a lawyer has to guard the transit. Meanwhile, broken friendship merely lies there in pieces on the floor. Society does not glue it back together or sweep up the remains. That is why friendship calls for infinite varieties of expression.

Recognizing a friend is the beginning of developing friendship. The great modern Jewish thinker Martin Buber, who wanted people to relate as "I" to "Thou," not "I" to "It," spells this all out in *The Knowledge of Man* in a passage which makes clear the terms of one person's encounter with another.

"I become aware of him . . ." My life had been going along on one course, and I may not even have felt the need to recognize another. But then my dull senses became alert in the presence of this other person. Like a birdwatcher who hears a new and strange call, or a fortune hunter who senses she is in the right zone, I begin with little more than a sensing.

PS 3.50*

FRIENDSHIP
MARTY M ARG 0895050536
PAPER ABK

089-505-0536 QTY______

FORTRESS CHURCH SUPPLY STORE
0340001 340023

10- 2-84

"Say, it would be fun to get together and talk one of these days . . ."

". . . *aware that he is different, essentially different from myself.*" All humans differ from each other, from their toeprints to the numbered hairs of their heads. But the differences show up most vividly in friends, since others cannot often discover what they see in each other. If they found perfect likenesses, their lives would remain cramped and narrow. But because someone else is essentially different, he or she can enlarge life for a friend.

". . . *different . . . in the definite, unique way which is peculiar to him.*" Just as one can find it easy to love humanity but not a particular human, so it is easy to talk about being a friend to *man* (the old-fashioned word for the human race) without being a friend to a particular human being. Illusion may persuade me that I have found a twin or a clone in someone else. Open eyes show me how different we are, and how good that is. But I had better learn early that in recognizing friends I do not get the chance to completely remake them. Let lovers try that with their spectacles and dreams, with which they would overlook flaws or recreate the beloved. In friendship, I must sooner or later learn to accept the uniqueness of someone who is going to stay much the way he is right now, no matter what I do. This person is already living well into an irreplaceable life script, and cannot tear it apart simply because I enter in Act Three.

". . . *and I accept whom I thus see . . .*" We associate acceptance with love and forgiveness more than with friendship. Paul Tillich, no saint at all, and

St. Paul behind him, taught us to think of God's action toward us as "accepting the unacceptable." The life of friendship is on a much humbler scale. We do not ordinarily become friends with the contemptible. We may love them, sacrifice for them, or be neighbors to them, but they are not our friends. The friend does not accept the utterly unacceptable person, but the individual of quality. This is the fact that prevents us from bringing out the great trumpets when speaking of friendship; it is not a purely selfless relation. But our lives are greatly enriched when we reach toward someone with attractive qualities, since these will never match our own. Sometimes they will shame us and just as often they will disappoint us. They will do this because the person who embodies them is definite, unique, and different from us. As friends we accept these differences.

". . . so that in full earnestness I can direct what I must say to him as the person he is." Here Buber displays a kind of sobriety or grimness that belongs more to encounter than to friendship. We often overcome confusions among friends with roaring laughs, not earnest conversation. Whispers over coffee, shouts at a soccer game, rib-jostling elbows, or the low-risk "Aw, come off it!" are often direct enough for our needs. Yet friendship meets its tests not only in our being with each other or through our gestures, but often in direct speech. Buber has it: "I must say to him. . . ." There are times when one cannot evade the eye-to-eye confrontation. But friends know that what they say in such earnest times sounds different between them than do editorials they read in papers or general statements about the human condition. "Harry, I hate to have to say this to you, of all people . . ." Such statements show that we know well who Harry is, and understand why our words must hurt him and jeopardize us. Because he is a friend, we can risk the word.

"Perhaps from time to time I must offer strict opposition to his view about the subject of our conversation." There it is. Opposition here, we must presume, has little to do with how her perfume offends the rest of us, or whether his taste in drummers shows him to be a slob to our crowd. Now and then serious people must be not only eye-to-eye but also toe-to-toe. The basic direction of another life, the root ideas, may seem to threaten the way we should be together and even the way the world should be put together. Here we picture fundamental divides: One friend believes in God and the other does not. One thinks that truth is one, finally to be agreed upon, based on absolutes on which all right-thinking people can agree. The other thinks that truth is many, or finally elusive, and that everything we can know is relative; life finds us with one foot on a banana peel and the other one also on a banana peel. Or one thinks that humans must be capable of sharing in the face of human need. Another would show no pity toward those who do not lift themselves by their bootstraps, whether or not they have boots. Friends do not let decades pass evading such subjects; they must confront them. They are friends precisely because of a mutual need they have to face up to such issues in personal ways.

"But I accept this person, the personal bearer of a conviction, in his definite being out of which his

conviction has grown. . . ." Disagreements between friends do not end in chummy promises to tolerate each other's views. On these terms, toleration is too wishy-washy a term to survive the demands of friendship. Instead, to the degree that I realize why my deepest beliefs mean so much to me because they have grown with my "definite being," I must realize that so it is with her. How she looks at the universe is not a collection of grab bag items she shoplifted and went home to open. Instead they grew out of her place and point in history: Were her parents loving? Did she live through bombings in a war? Was she a second child? Is her face scarred? Has she long been unemployed? Did she meet Marxists on her year's assignment in Peru? Are her family refugees? When these questions which establish her "definite being" appear, I learn that her convictions are not casual and that I cannot uproot them without destroying her. Perhaps I can change them, though I shall be changed as she responds. So I accept this person.

"*I* affirm *the person I struggle with; I* struggle *with him as his partner; I* confirm *him.*" Translate *partner* to *friend,* and you have it. Friendship makes room for struggle, but because this struggle arises between friends, we keep saying yes in the face of positions we might otherwise abhor. And because we keep on saying yes, we help the partner, the friend, to grow even as we grow; we have the security of knowing that our "definite being," our uniqueness, meets the test of at least one other member in the human race. We are survivors together.

One of the most grace-full features of friendship, yet one of the most threatening to its survival, is the fact that people can take it for granted. Most of those

74

who are surrounded by friends seldom think about how much these sustain life. Like the grace of God itself, the gift of friendship in our lives is part of the undertone in the bass; it gives a grounding while the treble can fret and trill. It is part of the firm ground on which a person walks, so firm that she can dance without reflecting on her base. The friendly and be-friended person is free for neighbors, enemies, and people out there who at first appear only dimly on the screen of awareness.

When friendship disappears we suddenly become conscious of what it meant to us—as if the bass notes were gone and we had only aimless and unhar-monious notes left, as if the ground had dropped from beneath us. Without friends, we become more self-preoccupied and busy with the tasks of survival and relocating our identity.

Perhaps a friend betrays, and the friendless thenceforth finds few reasons for trust in the larger universe. Friends move away or are transferred. Finding ourselves in a strange environment, we busy ourselves and fuss. "I guess I'll move the television over here, and the sofa here. . . . No, maybe I'll put them back. . . . I guess I'll wash my hands. . . . Maybe if I went down to the coffee shop I could run into someone with whom to talk. . . . Too bad this room doesn't have a telephone; I hate to go out into the rain to find one. But surely I could think of some-one to call long-distance. Well . . . I guess there's nothing left but television. At least the late-night newscasters will call me 'friend.'"

Physical distance from friends only stimulates in us the friend-making interest. Even betrayals or momentary separations are something most people can endure. The fact of a betrayal or a desertion, however hard it is to take when first we become aware of it, still serves to remind us that we have a friend-making capacity. Someone once cared for us enough to build our confidence in that friend and in ourselves. We must have been on a shared wavelength with that other person, and the very ability we had to locate each other suggests that after the sadness diminishes we can begin to reassert that ability.

Awareness of friendship has to be most vivid among people who desire friends but who cannot find or keep them. Somehow their lives are too full without friends when the opportunities come, and they become empty in the long hours when friendship would matter most. Some lives are closed off. The calendar and schedule are too full. Even with other people, the person in question is thinking of the office, of tomorrow's agenda. Potential friends can at once spot the individual who might intellectually state his or her readiness to welcome friendship while not being truly open to the intrusions of friends.

When the friendless person becomes aware of his distance from others and the fact that he is enclosed upon himself, panic sets in. Instead of reorienting his life and rearranging priorities so that he can become open to others, he is tempted to seek an immediate solution. Almost frantically he sets out to make friends. Desperately he scans the want ads for their listing of social groups which promise contacts. These are compute-a-date centers. The problem is, he did not want a date; he wanted friendship. Shall he take dancing classes? They contrive situations in which romance can blossom, but it is not romance that he seeks. Membership in a club? What is next? Singles bars stimulate anything but friendship, and he knows that well enough to avoid giving them any chance at all. The people at work have lives of their own. So he gets a bit pushy, trying to make friends out of acquaintances he long has snubbed. They are suspicious, and turn their backs. The very effort to go shopping for friends works against itself.

The birth of friendship occurs not when one gets a telescope or periscope and starts scanning the horizon of acquaintance or looking above and beyond it. Instead it stands its best chance when there has been a renovation of the person, a move toward becoming open. When the first chink of openness appears in what has once been a closed-circle personality, friendship has a chance. And once it begins its work, more openness follows and the open circle grows. So do the friendships.

4

Openness to Friendships

Some people surround themselves with acquaintances, and envious onlookers imagine them capable of friendship on the easiest of terms. But being "the life of the party" is not at all like being a profound and deep friend. The observer is more likely to spot friends in a senior citizens' home than in a singles bar. Married couples who have enjoyed each other's presence through forty years are evidencing a friendship that the Born Entertainer at the fraternity house has never known and is not likely to know. Two shy roommates who have overcome solitude and who care about each other will go overlooked among the Beautiful People being snapped with their devotees by photographers for the Sunday paper. But the Beautiful People jet past each other and dispose of each other, as the roommates do not.

In some senses the ability to make friends and deepen friendship may be a gift of God much like

genius itself. Not everyone possesses it in the same measure. A woman gifted at writing music may compose her melodies consumed with a passion for music, while her back remains turned to other people. For the writer, the silence is never silent enough nor the night long enough during the creative session. But those who stand in awe of his genius or eagerly request his autograph are not waiting to become his friends. The athlete never has to buy the drinks during the years of his prime. People want to be seen around him, to be able to brag about how close he is to them. But the time for his personal decline will come, and the athlete may then see the claque disappear. Meanwhile, old Bleachers Bill and his friendly cronies will endure as warm companions for decades more.

While being able to be a friend is in part a gift, there are things one can do to become more open to friendship. Most efficiently stated, this means that one must become more open in general. Here is our thesis: The person or personality that is open becomes more "available" to the presence of the divine, more ready to respond to nature, more alert to the stirrings and jarrings of other people, and will develop a character that allows friends their own openings.

Having mentioned how I work surrounded by a library of 8,000 volumes and on a campus with 2,000,000 volumes, there is a danger that together we will think of nothing but the card catalogs, the spines of books, or an occasional dropped footnote. Presently, then, let us pause long enough to develop an intellectual companionship or spiritual friendship with one of the living souls who stood behind some of these books.

I am at the same disadvantage toward him as are the majority of my readers: I never made the personal acquaintance of the author. He was distant, older, important. Now he is dead. But that is an advantage for the present purpose, because there is no danger that I will be able to drop his name or act as if I have access which others do not have to his thought. What I know about him is in his books, which are open to all. Is he a "best friend" among those authors? There are others I could list. But on this subject, no one has done more that is of help.

The author is Gabriel Marcel, a modern French thinker technically called an existentialist, who fifty years ago experienced a conversion to Catholic Christianity. He was not a pure thinker in the sense that he closed himself up in a study and refined his theories systematically. A man of action and engagement, Marcel was "impure" enough to use a variety of genres to express his philosophy. He authored a number of plays. Many of his more profound thoughts he confided to some unsystematic journals, which are unsystematic because life is, too. He taught that days come to us with surprises and various beckonings, and that the open soul responds to them in different ways. Marcel was a pilgrim, a person on a journey of hope, an imparter of that hope to others as he strolled or climbed through the stages of life. He left behind books with compelling titles: *Creative Fidelity, Man Against Mass Society, The Mystery of Being*. These titles are only signals. We will not be citing them apart from each other, but will reach for the bookmarked pages along the way as we explore the meaning of true openness for friendship.

Because Marcel was a convert, he posed his thought against the reality of a Presence, a Thou whom we (and often he) call God. To single him out on the subject of friendship is not to say that those who do not realize this Presence—people who might call themselves atheists or agnostics, to say nothing of doubters—are excluded from the circle of friendships. Marcel did not turn his back on old acquaintances. He kept learning from those who were closed to the divine Thou. But for those who *do* claim to be aware of the Presence—which means the majority of us and our fellow-citizens, if we can believe the poll-takers and interviewers—there are resources here that we seldom draw upon in our belief and awareness.

Marcel's conception of the basis of friendship grew out of his specifically religious understanding of communion. He believed that our movement through faith, hope, and love to the divine Presence provides us with special grounds to be open to other humans. Let us examine this systematically.

Marcel saw the absence of hoping, first of all, as the great blight of people today. He devoted much attention to restoring it. He was careful to separate hope from some of its opposites and its cousins. Thus it had to stand against the great enemy, despair. Despair rises from the world of apartments which kill people, the high-rises of impersonal dimension. They and the great bureaucracies "close off the horizon on all sides" and make it difficult for the spirit to breathe or escape. Despair "plugs us up." So "the man who despairs is the one whose situation appears to be without exit." Nothing fresh can ever happen in the suffocating world of the despairing. Yet hope is born precisely in the presence of continuing threats of despair, just as faith is a fire that feeds on doubt. Such threats provide challenge, which leads to strength. Hope stares despair in the face, and offers "scandalously carefree grace."

The despairing person is one who has to calculate. Such a person has to exploit surrounding people in order to serve his own purposes as he gasps for air. Hope, on the other hand, is not calculating. It allows everything to occur in its own time. Thus it can be relaxed, and can say to the friend, "Take your time!" rather than constantly setting the terms for the relation.

No one would mistake it for its opposite, despair, but we must take care not to confuse hope with optimism. Optimism is our own human creation. The universe does not give us evidence that says what the optimist wants to hear, that everything will turn out all right. Optimism occurs within the merely mortal horizon, while hope speaks to us in the presence of death, which limits optimism.

Hope is also not desire, for desire demands that we possess someone or something. Many kinds of earthly loves are built mainly on such desiring. By their character, they ruin the possibility that friends may know hope as they need it if they are to face the future together. The hopeful person—here Marcel uses the example of a patriot who dies for his country—is strengthened by the confidence that he has pledged his life to the rightness of the cause, that

the divine Presence guarantees the value of his sacrifice.

Hope is a kind of trust. It calls for an openness to the Thou who is not a product of our own horizon. I trust that "Thou" will not betray me or destroy me. Marcel assigns to the Thou what later gets transferred in a broken but still positive way to one's friend: "I hope in thee for us" is his formula. Of course, one finally can say this only to God, who is the guarantor of all earthly assurances and hopes. "Thou [Tu] is in some manner the surety [guarantee] of this union which links us together, me to myself, or one to another, or the 'us' to the 'others.'"

Marcel next discusses this spirit of hope as it informs the theme of love, for love alone helps us stand up to death, which threatens everything we hold dear. Love is stronger than death. People pledge love, as if to say, "Whatever changes may intervene in what I see before me, you and I will persist as one." In a play, one of Marcel's characters says, "To say that one loves a being means, 'Thou, at least, thou shalt not die.'" Suggesting that this pledge is at the center of friendship would be overstating the case, yet the communion that occurs between friends is a commitment to the theme that love is stronger than death. "To love someone truly," says Marcel's *Journal*, "is to love him in God."

We hurry past love, which will have its own place later in our musings on friendship, to the theme of faith that lives in Marcel's book title *Creative Fidelity*. Faith-fulness is vital to friendship, since anything more than casual ties implies a promise. Marcel liked to quote Friedrich Nietzsche: "Man is the only being who makes promises." Humans see beyond the day and pledge something about tomorrow. Not everyone makes promises or keeps them, but creative fidelity is the mark of those who do, and they alone are the kinds of persons who will make friends. Everyone else will be only a user, a consumer of other people. Such persons may seem close to others, but only in a spirit that is "a stifling intimacy which prevents the soul not only from opening out, but from breathing." The embrace that looks like a tender hug has the strangling power of death.

In some of life's relations the way of creative fidelity involves a formal vow. We use the vow to help guarantee a marriage, or to make a commitment for certain vocations. While humans can hold to an ideal, they can only make a true vow before or to a person. Now friendship does not often call forth a vow. Of course, if you are typical, you can remember the time back in elementary school when you were insecure about whether your friend would stay with you through thick and thin. So you went out behind the barn and all but wet your pants with excitement after the tingling of slight pain as you pricked your fingers and let your blood flow into the body of the other. You became a "blood-brother" of—what was his name? You remember the event, not the person. The next day, someone else chose up the sides and you were lined up with a new blood brother.

If people later find such vows childish, they are also unnecessary on the scale at which mature friendships occur. Adults enter friendships freely, and make promises not in a solemn and set-aside way but by ways of life that find them interlocked. Yet these ways of life reflect our sense that even in friendship we are on sacred ground, together pointing to values that will outlive us. These values are at the base of our communion and thus of our friendship. An individual who has the reputation of breaking promises is closed off from friendship. Soon word spreads. That person is unreliable, no friend.

With all the possibility of a life of promise, why, we may ask, do people close themselves off from friends, from others, from the Other? Marcel is a good physician as he diagnoses the reasons for this puzzle. One of these reasons is the simple fact that from birth, all humans seem to be centered on their own egos. A friend is someone who recognizes that natural fact and then compensates for it by remaining steadfastly open. Of course, each of us creates certain zones in which we are necessarily preoccupied with our own survival, ourselves. But the closed-off person has no zone others can ever enter. "It is because the egoist confines his thought to himself that he is fundamentally in the dark about himself." He cannot know his real needs because he does not see himself in relation to anyone else.

A second Marcellian measure of what prevents us from being open is something he calls *crispation,* a word I was surprised to find also in English dictionaries. A leaf is crispated when it shrivels and curls. Once you could have seen light through its green translucency. Now it has become opaque. The snail also is crisped and curled inside its shell. So is the person who is turned in on her own schedule and so is the fanatic. Such people are incapable of being friends.

Marcel uses the term *encumbrance* to describe what closes us off perhaps most frequently and thus wards off friendship. We are weighed down, usually by a sense of our own importance. The celebrity is someone who spends a lifetime getting recognizable enough that he has to wear dark glasses to protect his privacy, and then complains that he has to wear them. Notice that he complains to his hangers-on, not to his friends. He has no friends. The encumbered person in academic life dies by degrees, earned and honorary, about which she informs you whenever she is losing an argument to an acquaintance. The encumbered person must keep up appearances, and becomes too busy with that to open up to anyone else. "To be unavailable is to be in some manner, not only occupied, but encumbered by the self." No one else can help carry such a weight—certainly not a friend.

If we ask ourselves who seems most available, it is not the self-important, crispated, encumbered person, but—surprise!—it is also not the snivelling or grovelling one. Being overhumble is a good way to drive off a possible friend. We all learn that the person who is sure of being unworthy of affection has little to give. I believe it was Erich Fromm who once traced the image of a worm through Christian piety. Because in one sad Psalm the writer in agony before God said he was a worm and no man, some of the pious thought they would be especially virtuous if they crawled around before God and other humans like worms. Fromm asked: Who wants to be loved by a worm (except another worm)? We want to be loved and held in regard by people of quality and integrity. Anyone else, we fear, will always be using us as mirrors in whose reflections they can wallow in their inadequacy and guilt.

Marcel calls the alternative to this attitude "self-presence." His words of definition are difficult but they deserve remembering. Self-presence is "the portion of creation which is in me, the gift which from all eternity has been given me of participating in the universal drama, of working, for example, to humanize the Earth. . . ." "A nice place to visit, but I wouldn't want to live there" are words for a world made up of self-engrossed people, or of people so unsure of themselves that they are busy having no time to welcome us as their guests.

To welcome: That is the theme of the receptive person. She has a home, a space, in which to create hospitality for me. One passes many houses without remembering them, for they are nondescript and seem determined to blend into the weeds and broken fences of the moral landscape. But then there is a home that displays the morale of the "self-present" person who welcomes us as we enter into its life.

This is the point at which a main theme of Marcel's comes to light, the theme that unites his thought as it bears on friendship. He speaks of *disponibilite,* a word for which every translator insists there is no translation before providing one: to be at the disposal of someone else, to be available, to be open to the other.

"Being available" does not mean having nothing to do, keeping an empty schedule or calendar, or being ready to jump out of the line of wallflowers when the first eligible person of the opposite sex

walks by for the dance. We find that we are really interested only in the availability of a person we would have expected to be encumbered. Such a person has reason to have depths. She keeps working at them. Her office door is not always open. She is reading and thinking, getting deeper so that she has more to give when she must respond.

Let me confess here—there has to be some place in this book for confession—that my own capability for friendship is most jeopardized at this point. For reasons over which I have no control—and it is important for me in my "crispation" to tell myself this—my schedule is a heavy one. In addition to the visible parts of my work, there is much correspondence. It is hard to describe the number of manuscripts one has to read or the recommendations one writes in my way of life. I know of no structural way to avoid this problem. Could I employ someone to turn correspondents away with form letters? Could I snob out acquaintances by refusing to read their writings as others once befriended me by reading mine? Or should I carve away at the vocation itself and, if so, what part of it? Which arm, I am tempted to ask, should I cut off?

Years ago a friend wrote an article pointing out this problem of mine. He mentioned that I often seem to be hurrying the conversation along as if nudging my companion too soon to the next topic. There is in such an attitude little of the "take your time" that friendship needs. I cannot prevent the phone from ringing while you are a guest, and I don't have the stature to pay no attention to it by hiring a butler to answer it or by not caring who is on the other end.

Time is short, so while we chat I flip through the mail and toss away some that has no claim on me. I speak autobiographically, and I speak also, no doubt, for many others like me. (Next week we've got to get organized. I'll keep working at the problem. . . .)

The person of true *disponibilite*, I have been trying to say, will be busy and may look preoccupied. His or her schedule is already full, and still I become one of the people who enters his or her horizon, making it fuller. But this person knows how to engage in creative schedule interruptions, sensing when someone else should intrude. Marcel liked to use banking terms to describe this very personal attitude. In his journal in 1922 he spoke of the idea of "opening a line of credit to . . ." as a basis for community and friendship. Some people live with a sense of a limited bank account that will get spent without replenishing itself. But the person who draws on deeper resources lives off the interest on that capital and can keep the line of credit open. In the end, my extension of this sort of credit demands that not what I have but what I am has to be on the line: "I put myself at the disposal of, or again, I make a fundamental engagement which bears not only on what I have, but on what I am." Such assets I can transfer.

Marcel believes that it is one's bodily presence that becomes available, even across the miles through correspondence or in the reading and writing of books. Disembodied ideas float. I may rearrange them intellectually and stay at a distance. But embodiments, as in the form of a friend, confront me and force me to rework life. Now it may be clear why in the chapter about the author it became so

94

important for me to clear a ground. As Seymour Cain noticed of Marcel, the "open" author has to make a call to possible fellow travelers, "waiting and hoping for their response, taking this common feeling to indicate that this is the true way into reality."

Maybe all that talk was merely the chatter of an encumbered professor, who was trying to become unencumbered by leaving his footnotes on the floor and walking forward with a proud *I*. But it may also have been a case study in what availability is like, or how an attitude of openness shows itself in people to whom it does not come naturally. You probably have had the experience of needing to hear a writer you had often read, even though you knew she was an inferior speaker. Why? You had to confirm her ideas in her bodily presence and appearance. You began then to be open for communion. Presence, noted Marcel, "reveals itself immediately and unmistakably in a look, a smile, an accent, a handshake."

What makes communion with a presence valuable is not that there is a strong personality that waits to overwhelm us. Instead, a presence is someone who "takes me into consideration, who is regarded as taking me into account." That is why we tend to reserve the capital *P* Presence for God as the Being who takes us into account. Then we use this as a simile for the way certain humans have done so.

My colleague Paul Ricoeur ties together these themes in a book on Marcel and applies them to our subject. He notices that Marcel uses the same word, "to participate," when he wants to connect us in communion with both the Presence and presence, Thou and thou, God and the friend. "The first image, the first approximation I have of the hold of being on me is the influx of being which friendship [*amitie*] arouses in the very heart of my existence. And the first outline of my own [openness] to being is my availability for my friend."

Though availability is the distinctive genius of people like Marcel, it is also something that in part can grow as we will it, or as we respond to the source of all that is open and growing, the Thou. We perfect its art by bodily attitudes, by signals that show us to be receptive, and by the way we shed our encumbrances or tear up our schedules when they stand in the way of our being open and available. Until we become available and open, friendship or, better, a friend, has no chance at all.

5

The Nature of
Being Friendly

Distinguishing between family members is harder
than sorting out people of different parts of the
world. The robes of the Arab and the business suit of
the Swede, to say nothing of the difference between
the dark hair of one and the light hair of another, help
me tell them apart. But when I come to Sweden,
sorting out the Andersons from the Swensons and the
Johnsons gets to be more difficult. And within one
clan, it is easy to blur the Andersons, since the girls all
look so much like each other. Only when I come to
know them well—for example, by falling in love
with one of them—do the importances of their super-
ficial differences stand out.

So with friendship. There is little danger that I will
confuse it with anger or justice or marketing. They all
have their place in the economy of life. But friendship stands up close to love. They belong to the same
clan and have family resemblances. The temptation

is thus to blur and blend them before I find how valuable the differences between the two are. In comparisons, especially when the great thinkers are doing the sizing up, friendship usually loses out as the pallid and dull sister. But love in a world without friendship would carry burdens that now it is free to set aside.

Friendship is an idea for the philosophers. It is vague, cloudy, and abstract compared to "being a friend" or "having a friend." The reason for its paleness is clear. When we think of friendship we are generalizing. When we think of someone being a friend, we have the particular someone in mind.

If I say *friend* I cannot dismiss from mind the childhood companion who was always ready with new activities. This child awakened my sense of wonder. Through his confidence in me I gained trust in a world. That friend has little in common with the one who knew to sit with me through the long night when my spouse was ill, or another who timed a call just right for the moment when I had to hear a serious verdict from a physician. And both of them mean something much different to me than the physician who sits back and takes pains to explain his findings and to reassure me as a patient. I may have forgotten the name of the child. I shall never forget the names of the friends who helped me through past crises. The doctor and I have a relation that does not end with his care or cure and my payment for services rendered.

To be a friend may mean to be the most important person in the world to someone else over a period of years. Some adults in the city who choose never to marry have a roommate or someone in the next building on whom they can count for social occasions and holidays. But each of those two persons needs others as well—a friend to ring up during a trip to a strange city, a friend with whom to go to dinner and with whom to relive college experiences. After takeoff the next day, the visitor may not think of that faraway friend again for months, but their relation is nourished by this brief reunion.

The character of relations differs in every case, and the people who are part of them are irreplaceable. That is precisely the point of being a friend: You fill a role that no one else can. A sexual partner may fill only one function in a person's life, by satisfying certain physical needs. An employer or employee might be a very replaceable functionary; any number of other people could play the role and no one would lose much. When we hire a professional, our relations can remain stiff and formal. Modern life could hardly continue if every transaction demanded a personal tie. We cannot walk to every company and have a chat with the collector in order to pay a bill. Efficiency demands that we be as remote and abstract as possible.

Friendship differs from all these other human connections because the friend is distinctive, unique. If I ask, "Who is your best friend?" you are likely to think of an individual at once. If we talk about our own circles of friends, you will picture a place where you get together: a dormitory, a bar, a country club, a church, each other's living rooms. Any mention or recall of such a place moves one almost instantly to the picture of faces. Such faces belong to this person who will understand if I have to cancel a tennis date,

to that one who always prefers a straight-back chair, and to another who likes to talk about the deep things of life. There is no chance that I will confuse the three in my mind just because someone brought up the general notion of friendship.

Each friendship has a special taste and character, and no guidebook could begin to help us map our way through the territories in which we explore friendship. One friend is very happy with an occasional phone call while another is put off if we are so remote as to phone or write but never drop in. One friend insists on paying the bill, so we have to be cunning to catch the waiter's eye first. Another has what we used to call "shell-out falter," and can always be found in the washroom, in the midst of a distracting conversation, or takes longest to fumble for bills when the tab comes. And while this practice tests our being together, most of the rest of us find the foible endearing, and admit to gossiping about it behind his back. How can we lump any two friends together in the category of friendship? To be sensitive to the special quality of each friendship is to learn the infinite riches of the life of friends.

For all the value we assign to having friends, society does not know how to recognize them formally. There are award banquets for hurdlers and hustlers in athletics and business. Schools know how to reward distinctions or donations with honorary degrees. The pope can dub you a Knight of the Holy Sepulchre and the Masons can give you the 33rd°. In the military there are generals and Distinguished Service Crosses, and the nation honors writers with the National Medal for Literature. Commercial interests have learned to exploit Mother's Day and

Father's Day. But it is hard to find ways to award people gifted with the art of being a friend. We may hope that the situation remains thus, not because we do not need models and exemplars, but because once we have found standards, we have begun to learn how to reduce the idea of being friends to a scheme. And what a friend does in the modern world is preserve uniqueness. All fingerprints and snowflakes may differ from each other, but from a distance they all look alike. From no distance will two friends look alike or play the same part in one's life. We might well honor each other for being good at the art of being friends, but we must avoid assigning categories and then looking around for people to fill them.

I like a line written by poet Rainer Maria von Rilke, penned in praise of love but perfectly appropriate to friendship: that "two solitudes protect and touch and greet each other." We may bring to our perception of human nature either of two opposing attitudes. According to one view, we are all self-existent, freaks of chemistry and physics, bundles of molecules and tissue. Therefore, social relations too must be more or less accidental or purely practical. The other position rests on the belief that people are made for each other, that we derive from Being, the All, God. Thus, taken together, we are expressions of a single body, as if we were cells that animate each other. How people begin to understand themselves determines most of the other decisions they make about their lives.

In discussing friendship, however, one need not begin by settling these issues of apartness or inter-

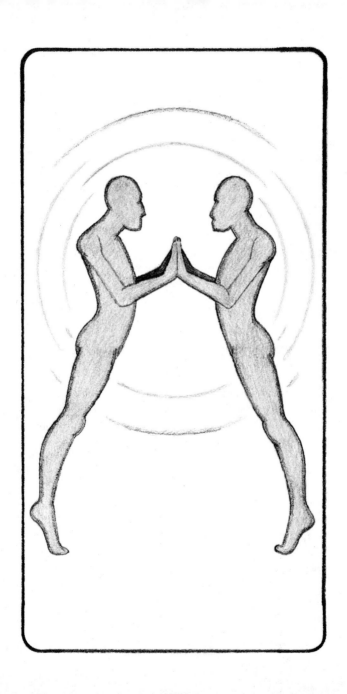

dependence. Both the self-existent and the mutually dependent know that in practice, life often involves great solitude. Humans have a private side and need zones of privacy. Self-destructive acts may set us apart from other people, causing them to shun us, or even from our own deeper selves, with whom we will have to come to terms. It is then that "having a friend" is as important as "falling in love." But falling in love can be a grand project, so absorbing that climbing out of it back into the human circle is difficult. One plus one equals one in love's intention. Friendship is on a different scale. Two solitudes "protect and touch and greet each other" without much danger of closing themselves off. The friend protects enough that a wounded person can regather strength, touches enough that the uncaressed feels the tickle and tease of the human bond, and speaks to offer a first sign of the great yes that the human venture keeps before us as a possibility. Since great love may lead one to be engrossed in only one other person, friendship, with its possibilities for multiplication, provides more hooks and tentacles on which one can rely until bleak solitude disappears.

Friendship may not rank with love among the great ideas or deepest themes in philosophy, but this does not make it of no importance. Some thinkers speak of "second-order" themes. Thus, a philosopher would want to deal with the "first-order" question of the existence of God before moving on to a second-order question as to how the grace of God comes to humans. But most humans devote more attention to being graced than to talking about the logic of divine existence. So it is with being a friend in relation to being loved. Certainly any thoughtful person would give first-order rank to the notion or experience of a God reaching across infinite distance to mortals in a created world and loving them when they do not deserve it. Without the reality of God being love, thought about humans being friends would mean little to someone who is restless for the divine. But never knowing a human friend might well make it hard for a person to resolve the questions of whether or how God loves.

Here is my crucial point: Composer Johann Sebastian Bach once wrote of music that it was a gift of God to the children of God, something for sorrowing creatures to give them a joy worthy of their destiny. We should think of friendship in similar terms. Friendship does not give the children of God their destiny, but like music, it is still a gift in the midst of their sorrows, a joy that matches their status as God's children.

If the existence of friendship is viewed as a gift from God, the human experience of friendship has something in common with one way we relate to God—through rite and liturgy. That does not mean that the friend becomes the object of worship, an idol. Such an obsession would warp friendship, turning it into persistent and perverse love. Friendship, unlike that kind of idol-making, is distinctive because it encourages a recognition of the flaws in the other. Friends unburden themselves. They agree and then they disagree. They find something in the other to like and much to dislike. Worshipful love, on the other hand, blinds itself to flaws.

No, friendship has a tone like the rite, but nothing like the object of the rite in worship. A great German

student of Christian liturgy once pondered what went on when people did something so unnecessary for daily work as stopping to kneel, to sing, to pray, to eat bread and drink wine together, to meditate. What they did was not "useful." It did not help them punch time clocks or produce more paper clips, to win more races or to get more raises, though in modern times some exploiters of worship engaged in misleading advertising by suggesting that it did. This scholar, Romano Guardini, noted something different about useless worship.

To Guardini, liturgy is "pointless but significant." So it is with friendship. In many respects it is pointless. Of course, we have seen that having a friend may possibly be a good form of life insurance, since loneliness can kill. And being a friend can produce rewards and yields for the day when one is sick and would like to count on another to bring the chicken soup. But a person whose eye is on the investment or the usefulness of the other is not being a friend or having a friend. Instead, such a person is only a consumer, a user who grinds up relations or hoards them.

Friendship, then, is *pointless*. It is born of emotions one does not quite understand, toward ends that one cannot at all foresee. One is as likely to be inconvenienced by a friend as aided by her. While one employer might recognize a productive sense of well-being in befriending an employee, many bosses would doubtless feel that such a relation promoted competition between friend and firm for the employee's attention. But if being a friend is pointless, it is also significant. It "signs" something. It signs that aspect of life in which not everything belongs to the time clock and the drill press, the starting gun or the annual bonus.

Friendship is *significant* because it signs the fact that some things in life are too valuable to be bartered over or put up for contract. One does not ask what can be gotten out of any kind of friendship worth having. Instead, the friend furnishes proof that in a world of betrayals there are reasons for trust. In a world of solitudes, there is space for protecting, touching, and greeting. Whether one finds such signaling in a barrio in Rio or among the fortunate few in a North American high-rise, it works the same effect. Those who take no time or pains over friendship will scratch their heads over the pointlessness of it all. But anyone who has ever known a friend or been a friend may find almost nothing in life more significant.

I have read in C. S. Lewis, a rare modern Christian who has penned some memorable lines on friendship, that friendship is not natural. Little in our genes or our makeup supports it. Those who think it has to do with nothing more than the civil defense of animals or calculating beings might find it genetically natural. But those who resist "nothing buttery," who find that friendship goes far beyond the call of such duty, will more likely side with the miraculous idea. Sociobiologists may still say that all life exists so that "the selfish gene" can have its way. Therefore they must arrange their questions about friendship so that they will match the answer they already have. Yes, there are advantages for survival in having friends, not enemies. So one has friends. We are also told that what we have thought of as altruism is the way the selfish gene has of keeping on living and providing for a future. But considered that way altruism, being generous, and sharing are "nothing but" a higher form of selfishness.

On the premise of the selfish gene as the determiner of all history it is hard to do any refuting. But in actual experience, two friends very often are not prudential enough or calculating enough to understand their time together as mere self-preservation. Friendship comes to them as a gift, a grace. Being friends is a surprise that goes against their natural impulses. In some cultures people may live according to the dictates of the *caudillo*, a leader who must surround himself with "friends," just as in other cultures those who rise to the top do so by collecting money. But when leadership fails and hard times come, when enemies encroach or even when they merely call in the chips, the spirit of *caudillaje* fails. The dictator finds that "friendships" acquired in the interest of power are shallow. One can be bankrupt in the world of friends as in the world of money.

Someone has said that people do not make friends, they recognize them. That may not be a bad way to look at the beginning of friendship. In this respect it differs greatly from divine love. Such love, according to the Bible, has to begin with God's view of the world. That view sees human creatures as fallen. People who believe in following the biblical tradition have many different ways of looking at fallenness. Some of them picture it as the result of a primeval act by a first human pair, Adam and Eve, who rebelled against God and then passed on this

Original Sin to all who followed. Others simply speak of the fact that all people, for unaccountable reasons, fail to act responsibly. And still others go no further than to point and observe: No matter where one looks, human-caused misery and cruelty seem to be the fundamental facts about the human story.

On this scene, God reaches out in the gift of Jesus Christ, who embodies perfect love, and takes a new view of all humans who accept the gift. Through Jesus, God looks at people "in Christ," not for their own sakes. God sees the perfection of Christ as a robe over people who otherwise could not present themselves as good. Thus, one might say that *God does not find the object of love but creates it*. God does not recognize some humans as meriting love, but makes them lovable.

Not so with friendship, which differs so vastly from divine love. We have not been trying to see friendship as a picture of how things are between humans and their Maker. Instead we view it as a gift to God's otherwise sorrowing creatures, something that like bread is necessary *and* like music is a luxury, a gift to give God's sorrowing creatures a joy worthy of their destiny.

So we might well imagine the human race as being very rich in people who are potential friends. Let a surrounded person make a list of those who can be considered friends. It is always interesting to notice how many of them come across our mental screens— as they came into our lives—almost by accident. The unplanned circumstance of our being born in one place instead of another means that our friends are likely to be, say, Montanan and not Nigerian, Catholic instead of Protestant, black instead of white. There comes a day when we choose a college. I can remember that enterprise in the case of our sons. They showed little interest in the question until they were sixteen when, with some passion, they started exploring college catalogs. These great works of fiction lured them to places that they accepted or rejected in part because of freakish encounters during a visit. Finally they each settled on a place and went there. They could have been at a thousand others. At college they recognized the friends who will provide the cores of their circles for much of their adult lives.

You meet someone on a plane and exchange business cards. Soon you are golfing, and join the same club. You might not have been on that plane that day, and you might have been assigned seat 8C instead of 9D. Or on an impulse you sign up for a course in cooking and there converse with someone during a break. Soon you are comparing recipes and then sharing the products of your kitchens. Each of you opens the other to an exisiting circle of friends. You pop open a can of beer under the sun in the bleachers; you have done it a hundred afternoons before, only to leave the crowd having done nothing more than cheer alongside the others. But one day two other people pop their beers open and you begin conversing. They drop you off on their way home. You pick them up two weeks later. You become bleacher bums together, and now have been for a decade. You may have worked at developing all these friendships, but you did not "make" friends the way God makes objects of love. Instead, you "found" friends, you recognized qualities in them with which you were sympathetic.

In recognizing friends, people do not find only good qualities. They discover limits. It is hard to picture a friendship that is only idyllic, a relation in which the various partners do not sooner or later become frustrated or furious. I recall reading a novel in which a married couple insisted on absolute honesty. They decided that beginning on their honeymoon they would tell each other exactly what they were thinking at all times. It was a short honeymoon and the marriage ended right after that.

What if friends, having found each other and recognized qualities they admired, then decided to tell all? What if they could read each other's minds? They might soon find that the victims of their mind-reading were jealous of them, or distorted truths, or made bad comparisons. I used to suppose that nothing worse could happen than that. Yet Bertrand Russell, beginning at that point, once went on to say that there would be a second effect to such a magical power. The first effect would be the destruction of friendships. The second would be the indication that the world could not get along without people being friends. So people would take a second look, they would continue hunting for friends to recognize. And in this second round they would not build friendships on dream worlds. They would not need illusions. They would learn not to insist on higher standards for others than they held for living with themselves.

If you think about people who have been your friends for years, it is likely that you will be able to recall times when their flaws became especially visible. How, you may have thought, can we ever have started this friendship? You do not notice those faults in people down the street. You do not notice them precisely because you do not know the people. You have no reason to observe them closely, to be frustrated by their failures. Being close to a set of friends, then, is an activity that helps you join or rejoin the human race. The exposure of a short-coming is a sign of our human need to be friends, not a threat to the endurance of friendship.

When friends fall out, they must begin the task of repairing their relation, usually on the basis of whatever it was that they recognized in each other at the beginning. They get back to basics. This often means that some criticism is necessary. Should you find it hard to criticize a friend? Of course. If you find it easy, we have heard, that is the time not to do it. At such a moment the friend is vulnerable, and if we swoop in on them in their weakness, they cannot stand the assault. If, however, the "offender" sees that criticism is coming from someone who finds it hard to utter, there is a good chance that the friends will become only closer, more secure after the hard times.

I wonder whether love follows quite this track, because the lover is always ready to remake the beloved. Love is a high-risk game that exacts more from the partners than friendship. But friendship is not the same kind of relation; friends must constantly go looking for and discovering qualities in the other. On those terms, friendship makes more demands than does love, which so easily forgives and recreates. Perhaps we have made too much of *recognizing* the potential friend. If we go looking around the human race with eyes wide open, we are not likely to find one. We squint, we close one eye, we permit ourselves to suspend some standards and allow someone with faults to enter our world. To keep the friend thus found, we do not close both eyes to the faults, but we open them both. Only after the illusions go is friendship likely to survive.

With eyes wide open, friends have to work at relations. According to an old Jewish proverb, "A friend is one who warns you." This could mean that you are warned against danger, or against a wrong tendency in life. "Friend, better watch out; if you keep that up you'll become an addict . . ." But it can also mean that the friend warns you against patterns that could destroy your friendship, patterns that would make it hard for you to continue to recognize reasons for friendship. Being in the warning zone and fearing the end of friendship are signals; they help ensure that two people will not position themselves so that every threat is allowed to pile on every other one until things break. What William Jennings Bryan once said in international relations serves as an alert in more intimate zones of life: "There is nothing final between friends." They have amazing abilities to restoke, to quicken what looked like ashes but still has a glow. They have established little habits and rituals that make possible new beginnings.

I have stressed the importance of realism, an "eyes wide open" understanding of the friend's limits, to demonstrate that idealism or idolatry does not constitute friendship. Such a stress is necessary in our times. A century ago in his journals, Bronson Alcott penned an entry that shows the kind of error we make when we ascribe to human friendship qualities it is too limited to convey. His opening line terrifies:

"Friendship is the only religion possible to moderns."
Why? "Our God is a domestic God, and that fine
sentiment which binds persons to each other is the
only piety practical and efficient." As I read this, I
think: "What a claustrophobic world!" Denial of the
transcendent power of God's love leaves us with little
room to breathe.

Where is the radicality of a God confined to the
cramping terms of human friendships? To speak of
God is to break out of confinement. The God we
need, the only reality we can conceive as meriting the
syllable *God,* is anything but domestic. This God
takes clay and inspires it with the breath of life. That
is not the same thing as finding a friend. This same
God does not give up on fallible humans. They lie,
cheat, steal, and undercut friends. Yet God, who
cannot *recognize* qualities in them, *imparts* qualities
to them. God makes them into objects of love and
then into subjects who can pass along love. Friendship is a bonus that God throws into the deal, a gift
that goes along with divine goodness but is not the
basis for ties between humans and the divine. When
friendship becomes a religion, our picture of God is
too small, our expectations of human life too large to
endure the tests. Criticism between friends is bene-
ficial because it shatters idols and blows up false
altars. Only after such shattering can we understand
what friendship is.

In Sunday School we used to sing a flat but snappy
little hymn, "What a Friend We Have in Jesus."
There are a few lines in the gospels that suggest
reasons for thinking of the rabbi of Nazareth in those
terms. One passage presents the notion that there can

116

be no greater love than the kind expressed by a person who lays down his life for his friends. Since the lines were written after the followers had experienced the risen Jesus, there is no doubt that we are here being privileged to glimpse the past through their eyes and to see them interpreting his death as an act of friendship. But the heart of the passage is Jesus' claim that the gift of life is a gift of *love*. He did not say, "A greater sign of friendship no one can give than to die for friends." In the same passage he is quoted as saying that he will call us friends. But this is a bonus, a plus. It is not the basis of the bond between God through Jesus to humans.

Though it may sound perverse, we might well say, "what a Jesus we have in a friend." Yet this is not as shocking as the first hearing suggests. Many Christian thinkers of the past spoke in such apparently scandalous terms. Some of them urged us to be not only *as* Christ to the neighbor, but to be *a* Christ to him or her. To be a Christ did not mean that we had climbed into Godhead and achieved divine perfection. Being a Christ was conceivable because when God looked at us now, this looking occurred "in Christ." God saw not us and our flaws but the perfection of Christ, which was the divine gift to us.

To pursue such an idea may seem confusing and could carry us into bypaths of speculation and God-talk. But the biblical witness is sufficiently clear: Divine character is somehow to flow through fallible humans, even though they do not thenceforth become perfect. So it may be that when a friend forgives us and recreates the basis of friendship, something as deep as love has to be present. It breaks the bounds of ordinary relations of the sort on which friendship is built. That is why it is not nonsensical to say "what a Jesus we have in a friend;" it may better protect the character of sacrificial love than to sing "What a Friend We Have in Jesus."

The love we call erotic has an element that the old-fashioned psychologists would have called "carnal." That means that it belongs to the *carnus*, the flesh. This is the sphere of desire, the passion of one to unite with the body of the other, to possess and be possessed, to come toward ultimate communion. Desire is a creative urge with a very destructive underside. Many novelists and filmmakers have shown that erotic love has a demonic tinge. By *demonic* they would mean, and I mean, the negative underside of desire's urge to create. I want to show my love, but a full expression of it in the form of possessing the other may mean I overwhelm her and leave her nothing of her self. If I fail to do so, I may plunge into suicidal depression. Passion takes over, and I am blinded. The temptation to idolize my beloved and to exclude everyone else from the field of vision through desire is so strong that we can see why sages counseled people against being given over to erotic love. They also worried that when the passion died, as it must in the life of virtually everyone, the lover would suddenly see, *really* see. Only all the faults would remain, and thenceforth misery would replace love.

The human race will not give up on erotic love because of such risks, but people do not have to invest in only its one kind of intimate relation. Alongside it, friendship seems to fall between the cracks and fill them. We do not live only between love and hate, between passion and ignoring. Friendship allows for varieties of intimacy that most other relations do not know. It brings humans closer in touch with others. To know human nature, we need friends. We can know more than one person through its means, for while erotic passion blinds a lover to others, the knowledge of a wider range of humans comes through friendly knowledge of one other, then two, and then a circle. In friendship we are free to test loyalties and to grow in our ability to reach out. Through friendship, we disclose something of our inner being.

In all this talk about how friendship and love differ, we have danced around a danger zone, a kind of no-man's-land. The zone was created by one of the great books—some would say one of the great distortions—of twentieth-century religious thought. A Swedish bishop named Anders Nygren wrote *Agape and Eros*. Thanks to him, whoever writes on friendship is expected to throw stones through its figurative stained glass windows. This is because Nygren, in his intense concentration on the theme of love, left so little room for friendship. I do not intend to attack the book on those grounds, but to show instead that it deals with such a different topic that it hardly touches on friendship, except to help clear the air or our heads. I owe too much to the book, for all its faults, to throw many stones. True, it exaggerates, but it does so in the spirit of G. K. Chesterton, who once said that now and then we have to exaggerate in order to tell the truth.

Nygren believed that one could get at the root of thought by seeking the basic motifs of writers, and then by pushing their thought to extremes. The agenda for his 764 pages was the grandest theme for the human soul: How do God and the human come together? The bishop found that this coming together occurs only on God's terms and by the initiative God takes through *agape,* or divine love. This spontaneous or unmotivated form of love reaches humans who do not merit it. *Agape* assures them the security that comes with faith. They do not have to stay busy running around with figurative ladders on which to climb into heaven. They need no report cards or charts on which to record Brownie points. They do not have to saw away at the bars of the prison house. The door is open. It is the nature of God to give all.

Eros, on the other hand, is the kind of love that is human, full of passionate striving, and for Nygren unworthy to have a place in the bond between human beings and God. Nygren attacked those theological motifs that had come to distort the biblical message over the course of time by relying on *eros* to explain how man relates to God. The writers who celebrated *eros* took human forms of desire, whether for a friend or, more often, for an object of love, and used them as models of the way a person strives to deserve the love of God. If people thought they must deserve it, Nygren thought, they would ultimately be left insecure and grasping, unable to love or be loved without ulterior motives of gain or merit. Caught up in this striving, how could they be free to pass on *agape*-type love to other people? For Nygren the key biblical mandate is "Herein is love, not that we loved

God, but that He loved us." If we are to love others in something of the divine mode, we do so by passing on that spontaneous love of God—*agape.*

Father Martin D'Arcy formulated a vigorous response to Nygren in his book *The Mind and Heart of Love.* D'Arcy scores points when he catches Nygren making a few compromises in his exaggerated line and overlooking certain biblical references. But, fundamentally he recognizes that if we take a personal view of the matter, we have to acknowledge that it is never pure ideas that do the loving, but whole persons. People tangle together the pure love that God works through them, desire of the sort they have for their own spouses or their own necks, and the regard they have for a friend.

Much of the debate between Nygren and critics like D'Arcy does not concern us here. They retrace all the ancient writers of the church to discuss who best captures the flavor of the transaction between God and humans. How we respond to their conclusions will depend to some extent on our own previous hearing of the plot of grace or merit. The present task is to rescue from the debate only enough for the sake of locating friendship in relation to love, also and especially in the Christian scheme.

In his analysis of Nygren's thesis, D'Arcy isolated four themes that provide a helpful portrait of *agape* to which we can compare the special characteristics of friendship. Let us examine them briefly. First, *agape* is sponteneous and uncaused. Those qualities, we notice right away, cannot be ascribed to friendship; friendship is caused by something I find attractive in another person. Second, divine love is indifferent to human merit. Yet friendship has to

121

break when it bumps into someone who in no way merits it. Such a person we call an enemy, not a friend. Third, it is creative in that it makes something out of nothing. You and I are valued not for our own sakes but because we are objects of God's love. That notion cannot be applied to friendship, because with friends we make something out of something: We locate qualities in someone else that together we can enhance. Fourth, *agape* opens the door to fellowship with God. Friendship has no right or reason to make this claim.

In every case, *agape*-type love allows for no trace of the love that we associate with "desire" or "friendship," because they originate in humans, not in God. Friends meet as equals, yet our union with God is never with an equal. In addressing the nature of friendship we are thus asking a different question than was posed by Nygren and D'Arcy. Our talk of friendship is not designed to show humans how to find God, to get right, or to be saved. When we are talking exclusively about the divine initiative, the word and theme of *agape* is in order. Nygren sees this most drastically when he quotes a line used by the Protestant reformer Martin Luther from a debate in 1518. Since it is the key to my own fundamental distinction between human and divine love, please permit a line of Latin: *Amor Dei non invenit sed creat summ diligible, Amor Hominis fit a suo diligibili.* "The love of God does not find but it creates the object of its love; the love of the human is to seek what it finds to be attractive." Certainly there is no reason to pretend that friendship creates the object of its regard. We give other names to such a relation. You are my friend because something in you is attrac-

tive to me. Our ties may not be the noblest. Giving one's life for an enemy must count for more in human lore than giving the same life for a friend.

Nygren's statement of the distinction between *agape* and *eros* is certainly helpful when exploring subjects that have direct relevance to how people get right with God. But why must friendship be seen only in its relationship to the scheme of salvation? *Amor amicitiae*, or friendly love, comes up only four times in Nygren's 764 pages, and each time the author sneers as he passes by it. He quotes Plato, that "the object of friendship is to gain some good for oneself." Agreed. In *Lysis* Plato made clear that "the ground of friendship is purely and simply desire." That may not help one find God or grace, but it also does not taint the use of the gift of friendship any more than my desire to gain enjoyable sounds in music has to be tainted. Why cannot friendship just be itself, an aspect of life lived in the sight of God? Not everything on earth has to be used as a ladder for climbing to the divine Presence. Some things, friendship included, need room to be themselves. Friendship is a gift, a grace, a mark and measure of the God who often chooses to give us our daily bread, good weather, and good times. But we should not twist the meaning of these gifts by attempting to interpret them as vehicles that bring us to God.

Now that we have established the meaning of *agape* and its importance in the relationships between man and the divine and between humans themselves, we can turn to D'Arcy's examination of the desiring love Nygren calls *eros*. D'Arcy uses Aristotle to explore the virtues of friendship, and he shows us that this kind of love is more subtle than the simple striving and desiring by which Nygren characterizes it.

Aristotle defined three forms of friendship. One is indeed built on the desire for profit. A second grows from pleasure. But the third derives from what is permanent in us. This is what Marcel calls "self-presence," that element which connects us with the eternal. Aristotle admitted that the first kind of regard disappears when profits decline. The second is self-centered and fickle. But the third "is the friendship of men who are good, and alike in virtue; for these wish well alike to each other *qua* good, and they are good in themselves. . . . Those who wish well to their friends for their own sake are most truly friends. . . ."

Aristotle complicates the theme in the end by showing that even this love of what is permanent is a form of self-love. But we are not making the claim that friendly love and friendship are a means or a model of getting right with God, so we may attend to D'Arcy's contention that this is not self-centered love in any mean sense of the word.

Father D'Arcy rescues the territory of friendship and dignifies friendly love by citing a passage in the Fourth Gospel.

> This is my commandment; that you love one another as I have loved you. Greater love has no man than this, that a man lay down his life for his friends. You are my friends if you do what I command you. No longer do I call you servants, for the servant does not know what his master is doing; but I have called you friends, for all that I have heard from my Father I have made known to you (John 15:12-15).

These words express all that was highest in Jesus' earthly relations. In Jesus' self-presence he showed himself to be unencumbered and available. He was open to the disciples whom he called to be his friends. Of this passage, D'Arcy wrote: "There is no finishing touch needed to that discourse; it says everything that can be said of love, if we would know the heights to which it can attain, the love of God for man and how men through God's help can and should love their neighbor. . . . The picture is there, and it is the final masterpiece."

While I have chosen to keep the line between love and friend-making abilities sharp, they do overlap in some ways. The great difference between the two is that love creates its object, and friendship finds it. Of course, the love referred to in that formula is the unmotivated, pure reaching out of God to creatures. When love takes on legs and breathes among humans, it may indeed be like friendliness. To show how these themes overlap, I will comment on a classic passage on the subject. I am not the first to take the risks that come with running the two themes together. In a footnote, a Canadian professor named Donald Evans emboldened me to see the tie and to comment upon it. The passage comes from the hand of H. Richard Niebuhr, a titan among modern Christian thinkers, who assigned four characteristics to love.

First, "love is *rejoicing* over the existence of the beloved one; it is the desire that he be rather than not be." So with friendship. I do not celebrate the existence of an enemy; not only can I picture the world without that sniper or viper, I wish the world would complete itself without him or her. Similarly, my neighbor may come to me as a burden or a duty. Jesus has to command love for the neighbor, but reminds us that caring for the friend is natural. That is why he does not give it many points if we are thinking of a scorecard in the hand of God. *Anybody* can love a friend; loving the enemy is a test.

Our booklength point, however, is precisely this: We are not talking about a scorecard of God or human striving to look good in the divine scheme. Our concern is to rejoice over and to celebrate friendship as a gift handed over to creation, as free as rain and sun. So to think of the friend as one whose existence inspires rejoicing, to issue in praise of the being and not the non-being of someone else, is to affirm creation.

Such rejoicing is "longing for his presence when he is absent; it is happiness in the thought of him; it is profound satisfaction over everything that makes him great and glorious." I doubt whether the longing of friends is as deep or searing as the longing of parted and distant lovers. But on its own scale, this longing can profound. Read letters smuggled out to friends from concentration camp victims, and you will find such longings. The famous letters from prison that Dietrich Bonhoeffer, a victim of Hitler, wrote to his friend Eberhard Bethge are examples of this. They speak of a long-distance communion born of hearing a piece of music both loved, or a birdcall outside the window. Most of all, there is longing because Dietrich needs confirmation: He must test his wild new thoughts on a friend. And in this communion there is happiness despite distance.

Next, "love is *gratitude;* it is thankfulness for the existence of the beloved; it is the happy acceptance of every thing that he gives without the jealous feeling that the self ought to be able to do as much." This is the trickiest part of the paragraph. Friendship includes thankfulness that the friend exists, but, as we have noted, that is not the basis of the friendship. "I am surely thankful that you are my friend. Have I thanked you yet today for being friendly?" Niebuhr does not commit us to such a view. Instead he refers to a gratitude extended not to the friend but to the universe, the law of nature, or the will of God for the fact that the other exists.

These lines are tricky too because they imply the theme of jealousy. The friend may give so much that I feel jealous, insecure because I cannot return anything comparable. But if our relation is deep, it is possible to go beyond that jealousy. So ours is "a gratitude that does not seek equality; it is wonder over the other's gift of himself in companionship." *Wonder:* That says it all. The fact that the friend is open to my existence, able to affirm and confirm me, is something for which I have gratitude *not* to that friend, but to God, to existence itself.

Third, "love is *reverence;* it keeps its distance even as it draws near; it does not seek to absorb the other in the self or want to be absorbed by it; it rejoices in the otherness of the other." Niebuhr here refers to an ideal of divine love and not the everyday *eros*, erotic love between humans. They should not, but people *do* want to overcome distance, to absorb and be absorbed. The language of love poetry is about little except such merging. Here friendship, as a somewhat looser form of engagement, has an advantage over erotic love and passion. By nature it is not or need not be so exclusive; one has a circle of friends,

128

but only one great love—at least, one at a time! With friends we are free to come and go, to live our own lives. Still, we have all known people who try to be friends but cannot let us go. Our schedules are not our own. They make demands and want us to be there to fulfill every whim. Such friendships have lost the quality of reverence that lets the other be other.

Reverence "desires the beloved to be what he is and does not seek to refashion him into a replica of the self or to make him a means to the self's advancement." The impulse to refashion and duplicate one's self in another is a burden friendship cannot bear or outlast. Otherness is the key to friendship, and when it is granted no rights, there is no point to the relation. "Using" friends is the death of friendship: It implies that they do not exist for their own sakes but for what I can become by grinding them up or stepping on them.

"As reverence love is and seeks knowledge of the other, not by way of curiosity nor for the sake of gaining power but in rejoicing and in wonder." If you are my friend, you are not my god nor my idol. But from the way people have dealt with gods and the sacred I learn something of how to allow you the zone of distance you need. If I am busy researching your past and untrustingly snooping on you in the present, I threaten our relation. With a lover I am tempted to do this; it is another advantage of friendship that it allows for perspective. A friend is someone you can be irreverent with, but reverent about. You and your partner or circle can roar with laughter in each other's presence. You can poke fun and work out practical jokes that serve to show that you are insiders in each other's worlds: Let no outsider try them. But just as religious people whisper a bit as they step onto sacred soil, it is appropriate to think of friendship as a zone in which one falls silent "in rejoicing and in wonder."

Of reverence Niebuhr says, "In all such love there is an element of that 'holy fear' which is not a form of flight but rather deep respect for the otherness of the beloved and the profound unwillingness to violate his integrity." That passage translates as well to "friendship" and "friend" as it stays close to "love" and "beloved."

Finally, "love is *loyalty;* it is the willingness to let the self be destroyed rather than that the other cease to be; it is the commitment of the self by self-binding will to make the other great." At last, friendship looks like love, because it calls the self to be disposed to sacrifice for the sake of the other. But love is still a higher ethic with its insistence that this sacrifice be made for enemies and neighbors as well as for friends. According to the words of Jesus in the gospels, the individual who clings to existence dies, but the person who is ready to die will live. So rather than worry about the destruction implied in final loyalty, we do as well to look at the construction that goes on in day-to-day loyalty.

The modern world provides few arenas for testing our loyalty. Marriages dissolve rather easily. People find it possible to break vows as readily as they uncross their fingers. Lacking great causes and deep beliefs, many moderns give their loyalty to the state. Because most of them were born there and because it has power over them, they wave banners and flags, sing anthems, hound dissenters, expel the possibly disloyal, and kill traitors. Then, when another force within the state or a conqueror from beyond appears to have more guns and more power, the weak instantly transfer loyalty to those forces in an act of self-protection and fickleness.

Continuity matters little in life when so many want to be "now" people, to do their own thing in their own way. They do not connect with others except to use them. While friendships need not be undying, and while many should be allowed to fade, the deep ones call for a loyalty that is "self-binding" in order to "make the other great." Bonded, two friends become more than twice as strong as either of them is alone.

In comparing friendship to love, there are hazards that one will make claims that are stronger than friendship can bear, or that the comparison will dim our awareness of the radical, special nature of love. But after stating all the safeguards, one can tiptoe to the brink of definition and see *some* ways in which human friendship overlaps with expressions of divine love itself. Martin Buber took care not to overstate the case, choosing the rather careful word *simile* when he discussed this overlap. "The relation with man is the real simile of the relation with God; in it true address receives true response; except that in God's response everything, the universe, is made manifest in language."

To speak of address and response is the security against cheapening divine love. We cannot insist too often that divine love creates its object and friendship only locates it. But having said that, once more we buy a ticket to other means of throwing friendship against a big enough screen that people can see its power. A friend's relation to a friend is a "simile of the relation to God." This is where Niebuhr could call forth reverence in human relations. The pattern of address and response calls forth openness. God acts toward the whole universe, including my friend and me, so it is now of far greater expanse than before. But insofar as divine activity reaches me, it bears qualities which I can at least weakly simulate or hold up as a simile in my relations to the friend. At the base of this activity is the sense that together we have overcome aloneness, and are subsequently in a zone where care of others is potent.

6

Change

Life in villages and cities is life surrounded by people. When some permit themselves to become friends, they force change upon themselves and others. Every day friends have to respond to each other's gestures and words. At different stages in our lives, our friends play different roles for us. Just as friendships change, so do friends, as old ones pass and new ones come, or as we desert flighty new ones for durable old ones. Change of friends and change in friendships are great themes in the life script, and they call for daily attention. Having friends and being a friend must take place in a climate of change.

At the start of a friendship, people spend much time telling stories, testing the waters of mutual understanding. We are all driven to discover who we are and what we mean—the proverbial quest for identity—and it is only when two solitudes meet that personal identity emerges. Identity is social; we arrive at it through comparison, experience, and evaluation. The modern master on the theme of identity is Erik Erikson, who defines it in part as something in me which is continuous, on which you can count. If, in my response, I likewise find something continuous in you on which I can count, we have begun to answer who we are. People seek identity in order to know whom they can trust. And this discovery represents the great initial change that friendship brings to each of us.

The bonds of trust that friends forge form an alternative way to organize life, an underground network, while above ground, computers and bureaus line everything up. Most of life follows the contract. Someone says, "Sign here," so you sign, and they hold you to it. Friends might, at most, say "Put 'er there," and reach out a hand. But because they know who their friends are and have developed trust, they are not likely to become formal about agreements if they are far into their stories together.

People easily forget how valuable trust is for keeping life going. Those who have stepped off a boat or plane in a city where no one speaks their language know how disorienting life without trust can be. If the crowd around me and I cannot communicate we cannot easily find trust. I am friendless, and thus at the mercy of taxicab drivers who bid for me and my bags at the gate. How can I know where they will take me, or if they will "take me" for a ride and my money? And where will they dump me? Where the shadows are long, the streetlamps dim, and the night silence threatening? Will I stand there alone, without the keys for doors or hosts to greet me? What are those footsteps? And what does that sign say?

I enter a room. Is this an opium den of the sort that, I have read, existed in this strange place a century ago? Is it a hotel or a house of prostitution? How can I eat without a menu, and is this a menu? Whom can I ask about the customs of the place? Is this a den of thieves or merely a gathering place for people with full lives apart from mine? Are they sizing me up in order to loot me or (as I suspect) paying even less flattering attention by paying no attention at all?

Without trust or the means for finding it, I back off and hope to return unnoticed into the safer night. Still the street signs mean nothing, and I stumble. Dry-mouthed, I would cry out if I could as a hand touches my arm. This is it! Yes, it is; but "it" is the hand of the friend who was supposed to have met me at the gate, or near the spot where the cab driver let me off. This friend speaks my language. I have known her for years. The touch on my arm was gentle not because an enemy had to sneak up but because a friend did not want to startle. She knew I would trust her as soon as I saw whose hand it was.

This friend brings me to the inn where I was to go. Surprise! Our mutual friends are there. They have been waiting, hungry like me for another person who shares their stories and memories, who speaks their language. I know what is ahead. They will uncork the bottle and interpret the menu. Soon we will be laughing over my fears. There will be stern moments as they tell me which neighborhoods to avoid, and teacherly moments as they explain techniques for survival and enjoyment in my new setting. But most of all there will be a dropping of the guard, because we know we can trust each other.

In day-to-day life the importance of trust as a base or result of friendship hits everyone fortunate enough ever to have had a friend. You can remember how it was the first day of school, with the puzzling smells of rubber erasers and wide-lined tablets. You were afraid when one parent dropped you off in front of the forbidding building and the other withdrew the hand that held yours as a teacher took over. The bells that rang sounded alarm and doom. Where do I go next? Where's the bathroom? How can I get a drink? What if I fall out of line? Will someone slap me if I do something wrong? Will I get chosen when they choose up sides at playtime? Who will protect me from the bully? What is that strange language they are talking, about "registration" and "values" and "detention"? Let me out of here!

And then: the glimpse of someone familiar. More than familiar, a friend. You met the other student last summer in the park, but you did not know that her family had moved nearby and that you were going to be at school together. You find out now that she has been around for a day or two, since before school started, and she knows the ropes. She has friends who are "just waiting to meet you." Because they trust her, they give you a chance, and you find they are generous in enlarging their circle. You learn who you are and what school and its customs are because you had already learned friendship.

When you were a teen, someone sent you off to camp. Summer camp was as bewildering to you as the first day of school to the terrified child, or the dark streets of the strange city to the traveler. For an hour or two it seemed as if everyone else had been there forever. They knew how to find the best roommates and the best rooms. They knew where to be when, and which was the right food line. You flounder: Where is the snack bar, and who is in charge? Will they make fun of me if I miss something or am in the wrong place at the wrong time? I want to go home! And then a generous soul sees you in a world without trust and comes over. You find you have common interests. The venturesome one says, "I'm new here, too. My parents wouldn't let me go to a camp where my friends were. They said I needed a change. I also need a friend." So did you.

And you were off together, soon in the company of others. Until four in the morning you compared notes about home and school, and found that just before dropping off you were even able to admit how scared you'd been. The morning bell would ring too soon, but secretly you could not wait for it. You had friends with whom to play volleyball and kid around in the crafts room. You would be hiking together, and tomorrow night you would be telling more stories. You would even be able to suppress your homesickness during dreaded letter-writing hour. "Dear Mom and Dad: Camp is pretty good. I am making new friends . . ."

If we stress trust as a basis of friendship, we also have to stress mutuality. Friends must reciprocate; that is why what they are involved with is so risky. At the birth of friendship, someone has to reach out and create an opening, to call for an answer. That is fearful business, because few of us like to be rebuffed. And there will be rebuffs. Some of the people we would like to reach are unreachable. They are closed off, preoccupied with their own affairs.

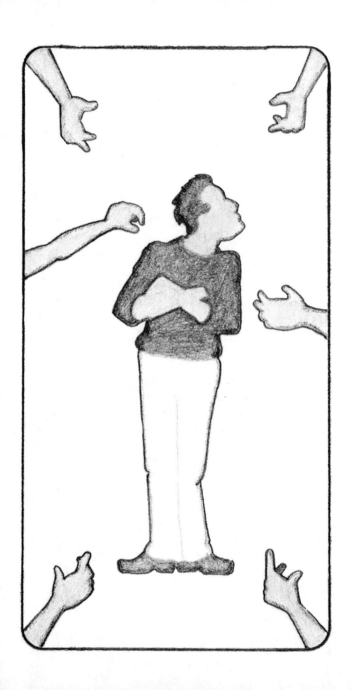

They have their friends, thank you, and do not need to pick up more encumbrances in a strange city, a school, or a summer camp. Their attitude creates no cracks for light to fall through, no openings that could enable a friend to jam a door further ajar. Their shrugs may not be malicious. Not all personality types interact easily, and you may not belong in each other's circles. No one says that everyone must be a friend to everyone else as they must be neighbors to all. You can wear out the gift of making deep friendships by being too inclusive. It is possible to interact with strangers and fellow students without becoming committed to long-term bonds. It is possible to be generous and courteous and then to move on. There are four billion people on earth, and it is sentimental to picture one's being able to enfold more than a few of them in trust relations. Cash registers will remain, and locks on doors. The world will still need bureaus and computers to run its crowds and their transactions. Let passing parades be passing parades. But as for you . . .

Here and there, now and then, surprising friendships will emerge to "give you a joy worthy of your destiny." So on occasion you expect reciprocation or you will reciprocate. In the divine pattern, love does not demand anything of this sort. God loves the unlovable, and creates attractiveness in the unattractive object of love. Of course, the recipient of such love will want to respond, but no response matches the measure of the divine gift. And even human love, as between spouses or lovers, is not necessarily reciprocal in every respect. But when friendship comes up, everything becomes different. When Jesus calls disciples *friends* in a gospel account, there is pathos if they do not befriend him in turn. We cannot picture the famed Beloved Disciple, a mysterious figure in one of the gospels, not knowing that something is expected of him. Maybe in calling for a friend, Jesus is doing something different than when the gospels show him dispensing his Father's love: Jesus is awaiting a sign of something special inside the friend, something that makes that friend attractive to him.

It is said that Jesus named John that special friend, the Beloved Disciple. This did not mean that John became secretary of state or foreign policy adviser. Maybe John was the jokester, the one who knew how to make the others laugh. He did not have pull with Jesus when it came to handing out authority. For that, Peter seemed to be the trusted one, even if he eventually betrayed that trust. But in gospel accounts, it was to friend John that Jesus entrusted his mother. We picture John's readiness, his eagerness to reciprocate for the acts of friendship that Jesus had shown him. We picture Peter being blustery, eager to please, ready to speak up, but not necessarily the one you'd like to finish off the wine with after the publicans and sinners have gone home to their friends and you are left with your own.

Reciprocity does not mean dependency. A counselor does not necessarily make a good friend, especially if I depend on his or her advice for straightening out my messed-up life. Why? I have told my secrets, and the counselor has them stored up. But an adviser need only dispense enough to keep the conversation going. The person I consult can withhold herself, can set the terms of our relation. She may do much for me, but her necessary reserve in our meetings for therapy keeps me from becoming independent enough to meet her as a friend on friendship's terms.

While friendship is built on trust and demands reciprocity, it is not based on thanks and does not expect constant gratitude. If you have to say *Thanks* all the time, you are not dealing with a friend. Of course, it is necessary now and then to put into words the unspokens of our lives, so a friend may be lifted to hear such a word. But for the most part, trust between friends is such that one need not keep balanced books or accounts of how often there are favors or voiced thanks for favors.

Circles of friendship are also not fan clubs. Naturally there will be a magnet person in the center of such circles. Someone there has a gift for generating company and before long a cluster gathers. The members genuinely become friends. But unless they are careful, a subtle change can occur and the pre-eminent one may be placed on a pedestal. The others do favors and bow low. Before long they are unable to do what friends are there to do: to prick the pretensions, to laugh at the wrong and thus the really right time, and to ask, "This time, friend, haven't you gone too far?" And when no one can ask that question, the friends have all departed and only devotees and fawning courtiers remain.

In the spiritual life it may well be true, it must be true: It is more blessed to give than to receive. But in the spiritual life of the sort that gives strength to friendship, it is at least as blessed to receive as to give. Certain partners in friendship at first by design and then by habit press themselves upon the others with gifts and errands. The familiar stereotype of the Jewish mother fits this pattern: She gives, gives, gives and smothers with affection. But the child has the feeling that she is keeping a scorecard and always stands ready to exact a reward in the form of life-long fealty. "The least you could do is show your mother some love!" You do not have to be Jewish or female to live into that stereotype. People of all races, religions, ethnic groups, classes, and relationships are democratically capable of embodying it.

Especially friends. "Can I pick you up to go to the ballgame?" "Oh, no, I'll come by again; why should we break the pattern?" "Here, let me buy this round of brats and beer!" "Not on your life. It's my treat. It always is." So go the exchanges, as one friend dominates. What is on his mind? Is he naturally generous? If so, why does he not spread his favors around to people who really need them? Only close friends get in on the largess. Is he keeping score, piling up debts, extending some chips that he will call in one day when I am least ready for it? What inner insecurity prevents him from letting someone else get caught up with him in the balance of favors? Your guard goes up at once. Dare you let this web encircle you? Is this a friend, or an automaton of sorts who has become expert at doing things for others without letting another person change his life?

Insisting that one is not keeping score is a way of keeping score: It forces all those on the receiving end to busy themselves all the time. They dare not let themselves become dependent and, by associating with Mr. Largess, begin to lose their own ability to spread the gifts of friendship. Soon, some friends declare their independence from the gushy giver.

143

Others drift quietly away. Some inner deficiency has shown itself in the "philanthropist;" the individual who would like to be a friend but is unwilling to be befriended finds himself alone.

"Why did everyone desert me? I did *everything* for them. I picked them up for ballgames, and I bought the hot dogs. Never did I let a birthday go by without sending a card. I can't remember ever forgetting to do something for them. They aren't very grateful; that tells me a lot about human nature. There must be something wrong with them. They don't even know how to let someone befriend them." Words like those are spoken into a mirror; we bounce them off the walls of our own little rooms. By the time we utter them, no one is left to hear. We have not been available to other people, who have their own needs to give.

While friendship builds on what is continuous in life, for the sake of trust, it also is healthiest if it challenges people to change. Of course, one of the pleasures of a longtime relation lies in the security we feel upon recalling "old times" and "old friends" and "old, old stories." If you are at least middle-aged, you have probably had the experience of coming across intimates of long ago at an airport or a convention. You find yourself instantly in communion; it is as if years had not passed. There may be much catching up to do: You compare waistlines and hairlines, sagging profiles and hairdos. If the years have been long and you have families, you may soon be comparing pictures of children and grandchildren. But you do not have to rebuild trust. Such comings together allow for almost instant unbending. Insofar as change comes into play, it hangs over the conversation as an unwelcome guest. The gray strands in the hair, the deepened lines around the eyes, the tear that comes as you speak of a friend gone or a love demolished—all these have a mark of death, the change that means decay. And you welcome the shelter friendship provides, because not all the storm reaches you at once.

Aspects of more positive change belong to active friendship. Many a family room wall displays a poster that carries the nudge of John Newman: "In a higher world it is otherwise, but here below to live is to change, and to be perfect is to have changed often." And yet the people who have these lines in memory will not automatically welcome change, even if it means growth. They might as well have a line of Richard Hooker's on the opposite wall: "All change is inconveniencing, including change from worse to better." We grow accustomed to the easy chairs that conform to our rumps, and find them refuges from action. Even the darkness in our own minds and rooms does not threaten, precisely because it is our *own* darkness. It is hard to get up for action, discomforting to turn on a light that, while it illumines, causes us to blink and commits us to seeing.

Much of our fear of change is fear of going it alone. In the bleakest sense, saying good-bye is a mark of death, a practice of it. Will friends remain open to me even when we are apart? "Drop me a line now and then, will you? . . . Give me a buzz if you have time, will you?" Eventually the lines come with more spaces between nows and thens, and the buzzes find less time, until the former friends drift apart. But friendship is a training ground for such changes; it prepares the adept to find new friends and to treasure the occasional thought of others across the miles. The distant friends, from whom one hears annually or accidentally at greater removes of time, play one role. They serve as landmarks, as points for comparison. These friends provide consistent voices against which to measure our inconsistencies and our growth.

The friend up close has a different responsibility. Having your best interests at heart, she can caution you when you are ready for foolish change. It would be nice if a friend were always available to remind you that no single therapy is going to make a new person out of you instantly. Change is subtler, more expensive than that. Of course, you can experiment with shortcuts: You may indulge in Primal Scream. You can make the quest for the Perfect Martini or the Perfect Orgasm your Holy Grail. You may join this cult or that T-group, sip all the right elixirs, and learn all the code words. You might even expect change in all respects because you were "born again" or "had the experience of the Holy Spirit." And yet you will lapse, and growth may be slow. People who are SOBs, as only their best friends have a right to call them, often remain SOBs in spite of themselves if they risk everything on the long shot of instant change. Friends do well to warn them off.

Do I dare? some ask. There are more people who resist change for fear of the unknown than there are desperados seeking to make raids for instant change. And here too a friend can provide the nudge. You might argue that your friend can provoke experiment because "it's not his life he's taking the risk

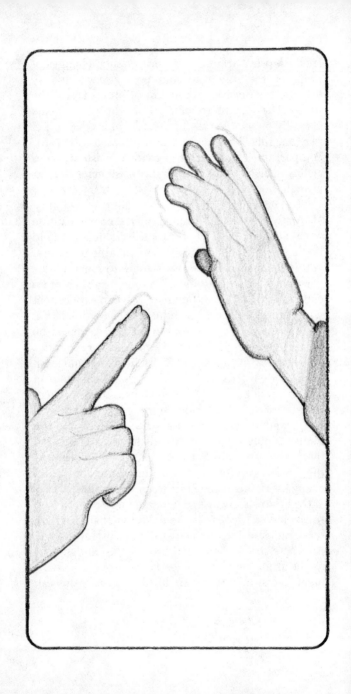

with." In some ways, no. But your friend *does* take risks in such situations. If you fail, he will lose something, for he has an emotional investment in your success. But a friend can view your problem with a bit of distance and a perspective you lack.

Most inducement for change does not come from friends concerned that you are staking too much on the cure-all of instant therapy or standing off from an important decision out of fear. Friends interact also on more mundane levels, through subtle choices they must make alone or together. In the most profound sense, the actions of the friend demand response. She suggests that we stop hanging out with this crowd and go with that one. He wonders what we think of this wine or that music, and we have to commit ourselves: Will we come on as slobs or savants? They want us to enroll with their group in First Aid, and we have not had time for such things. Will I stop smoking because my friends are irritated, or start smoking because they think the stuff they have will give me a new thrill?

All these positive and negative signs call for response. They disrupt the trajectory I had set for my life, they are planned forays on my security. When I hear of such calls, I think of the life motto of Eugen Rosenstock-Huessy, the marvellous modern thinker introduced in chapter two. This European expatriate to a Vermont village left behind the Daimler-Benz factories and the European universities in the interest of inventing work camps and clusters where people met face to face. His motto read *respondeo etsi mutabor*, "I respond although I will be changed." True response comes from so deep in my being that as it erupts I am shaken. Then there is room for new planting or growth.

Sit on a log and think about valuable changes that have occurred in your life, and you are likely to find that they came because of a response to something you did not seek. Maybe you were moved to response when a nation called you to service, or when a church asked you to speak up. The call of Jesus Christ to discipleship, and with it to death and life, disrupted what tax-collectors and you had planned by way of career. An emergency call at night from an alcoholic lifted you out of anonymity and you had to hear a long story before you called that person to surrender and start over. Alma mater was in trouble. You found it easy to turn down mailed appeals, and even phonathons. But a friend beckoned, stated the case, and not simply to look good in her eyes, you coughed up funds or signed up for a new cause. In each case someone or something called for a *yes,* and having risked that yes, you had to follow up on its consequences.

Sitting on that log a little longer, you are likely to find, in your catalog of reminiscences, that more often than not the calls that led to change came from friends. The nation demanded that you be drafted. The church made broad appeals. Alma mater worked with computers and mailing lists. In response you went grudgingly to war and came back having had new experiences but without experiencing change. You licked the envelopes for a churchly cause and maybe even said a prayer, but you withheld yourself. You wore the old school tie long enough for the fund drive but not long enough to keep on caring.

When a friend called for response, however, *although* you had to be changed, you answered. Again, the old trust relation carried you through— and you came through for your friend. In addition to this enduring continuity, though, friendship bases itself in the future. You and the friend intend to keep your relation, to check up without keeping score on "how we're doing." Are you faithful to commitments? As you try to fulfill them, what are the high and low points in your life? The friend has a hold on you that the paid solicitor does not. And when you thin out in your response, it is the friend who can come back again and can expect the same response, as the mailman cannot.

Drab friends are not able to issue calls for change. They will not test you because they have given up on the world and on both of you. But in almost all circles there is someone who has not let imagination die just because society wanted to kill it off. I have an artist friend who causes me to see because he knows what surprise is. What he knows could perhaps be put in a book, which I could read without making a commitment to see. But he has something else in mind.

This friend, who knows what I am missing because I do not see, takes me along to a small town on the plains. I have looked it over a thousand times, and overlooked it every time. One could easily drive right past. Ask the inhabitants, and they will say that Jake Knapp's house is the nice one. As a matter of fact, it is. My friend reminded me that the great novelist and photographer Wright Morris had once come to my childhood hometown to take pictures of eggs in buckets, overalls hung on pegs, drab wallpaper, piles of tires, and Model T Fords, and I

151

wanted to follow up: So I talked to the postmistress, an occupational gatekeeper to the larger society. "Oh, Mr. Morris? Yes, he was here, but he didn't take any pretty pictures. He drove right past Jake Knapp's nice big house."

But Morris has shown us something in those less attractive objects. And now the artist, who is a friend, wants me to grow, to see as Morris saw. I bring along my Instamatic. The artist teaches me how to line up the verticals of the great grain elevator against the sky. Have I ever noticed what happens as I let the three railroad tracks find themselves infinitely narrowing against the horizon? And had I ever let the heat waves that rise from them make me dizzy before? There! he points, and I am to see the dribble of oil on the puddle. Yes, I know that it creates iridescence, but it is, after all, nothing but ugly old oil on a black glop of water. To my artist friend, who is changing me and calling for response, there is no room for "nothing but" in the universe. Stoop down. Look at the colors. Remember the slide he took at a similar range? Here is the rainbow which I would have called beautiful against the sky, but splash away with heavy boots as we walk the streets of the town. And, by the way, did I hear the warbler in the distance? No, as a matter of fact, I did not. I was bent over examining oil puddles, too busy to let my ear work as well.

Safe enough, that scene. But another friend may call for response when she drags me along to a meeting of people on the other side of an issue I believe I have settled. I do not have to respond. The group and its ideological enemies have already reached me with bumper stickers. Either I am a murderer, because abortion is murder, or I am for choice, because a woman's body is her own, to do with as she likes. While both are rather slipshod statements of philosophical conclusions, they are still in the zone of philosophy, of ideas.

Once inside, however, my friend surprises me by showing where she stands on the issues. And now they are not abstract issues, because before me is a person who feels deeply about them. Perhaps she has had an abortion and has lived with enough guilt that she must exorcise it. Back then, she had been casual about her body being her own to do with as she pleased. Now she is not sure that a body is a thing that a woman owns, or that she owns it apart from people to whom she is close. And she is confiding her unease to me. Or she has invited me to this meeting because of a terrible trauma. Not believing in abortion, she talked a woman friend into letting a fetus come to full term against all medical advice. Her friend lost her life in the process. She reaches out to me for a comment: Are her conclusion and commitment right? And I had thought I had my mind made up. Now I must respond, although I will be changed. That does not mean that I sentimentalize the relation and toss creeds and codes aside. It does mean that creeds and codes take on a different color when I deal with the living soul.

At the end of the encounter, we may disagree. Half the time we would have to disagree, for the causes oppose each other and both cannot be right, or right for all friends and me. But we have by a call for response moved beyond trivial friendship. We can test our deepest beliefs because, as John Courtney Murray said of people in civil society, we are "locked together," whether for civil disagreement or agreement. Agreement may never come. Even disagreement involves a struggle—it is hard to determine just where our convictions diverge and clash. Confusion and chaos are easy to settle for. But friends exist to raise hard issues, to clarify them, to keep the language alive so that human care can grow.

Because friendship reveals so much about life, it also casts light on the rhythm between the old and the new, between traditional and novel, between what is continuous in life and what needs invention. I refer here to the special functions of "old friends" and "new friends."

Old friends are the best friends, we say on many a day. Sometimes this is a sentimental expression of people whose outlook on life is dimmed and whose sense of adventure is half-lost. Old friends, we presume, make fewer demands. Or we have known them so long that they stand no chance of penetrating us enough to cause second thoughts about anything. They may represent threats, but we know their limits; after ten years or forty, they are not likely to explode. If they do, we blow away the volcanic ash and go about our business, letting them know that we are not likely to be upset by such tumult.

Old friends play a special part in the economy of relations. Negatively, they can serve as governors. If I am typical, I can testify to that. While not a celebrity or a household word, I have seen my name in print and smiled from ear to ear carrying an award home. Sometimes awards come when we are all lined up in the formal robes of the academy. People who talk in English that sounds like Latin grace these ceremonies with prose that recipients are in danger of taking seriously. We march in long lines, the circumstances of which induce pomp. The bands play. What a great man am I. I am tempted to start getting formal. Maybe I should clear my throat and fake credentials from Mount Olympus. The world has been waiting for my classic. Let me sound important and it will issue forth from the gods, just as I did.

Then along comes an old friend. You know the type and the tone. "Congratulations. Let's toast you." And as you sit down to a festive meal with such friends, in no time at all the reminiscences reach back to high school or college days. And you know that they know that you know they have "evidence" against you. They know the stories about your days of raising Cain, your adolescent experiments, the practical jokes you pulled or had pulled on you. They did not take you too seriously then and have good reasons not to change their minds, among other reasons because they know your limits and because they have their achievements as well. And you have the goods on them. I have a friend who knows that once in alliance with a prankster (and in total fear of the linoleum-cutter he carried in his pocket) I was an unindicted co-conspirator in an act that led to the flooding of three levels of a dormitory to rug depth. This friend entered a blood oath alliance not to tell, since his telling would have meant my expulsion from the prep school. In my mind, my participation was an act born of fear. But my friend knows enough about repression in psychology to realize that I might have revised my motives after the act. He has always thought there was a wink in my eye and delight in my voice as we helped mop up the watery mess in the dormitories so long ago.

Old friends know how embarrassing were the early poems, how foolish the first ambitions to write. They know the times the joke was on me, or the times we got into scrapes together or were just plain foolish about human relations. Any temptation to suggest that I might read the laudatory publicity of a later year seriously will be met by something only the old friend can do with effect: "Aw, come off it."

I tell that story in order to trigger similar recalls in others. I think of the countless times that teenagers about to receive a sermon find their necks saved by an old friend of the scolding parent. "Listen, kid, it was 1:00 a.m. when you came in last night. I've had enough of it. Why, when I was young . . ." Then, suddenly, the parent becomes aware of the friend, an old friend, standing nearby. And he knows the friend remembers the 2:00 a.m. escapades years ago. So the tone changes: "Ummmm . . . Take it a bit easier; you had your Mom worried last night."

I used to think we did not learn the age of motion picture or television stars because they wanted to play the futile game of hiding the devastation of the years. Maybe old-fashioned pride or the worship of youth are part of it. But just as important is the desire to make it hard for us to locate the old school year-book, and through it the acquaintances who were once friends. These old friends remember the days when Miss Big was rather small. To know the story of a person's past is to have power over and to limit that person. If one can apparently spring full-grown from the foreheads of the gods to the pages of *People* magazine, there is less danger that old follies and furies will come to light. So the only kind of relations such journals can show belong to the "now." Old friends have been ground up or put on ice along with old spouses and old benefactors.

On the positive side, we work at old friend relations for as many reasons. They are not needed on the days when success leads to pride so much as when failure tempts us to despair. The old friend is someone with whom we have weathered trials together. We would not be friends had we not seen bad times together, unless either of us lived in a utopia beyond human disappointment. We gain credentials to remain in each other's elect circles by the times we have interrupted our schedules to be at each other's side. We know them so well, and they us, that each can detect in the other emotions that the other is not yet ready to face. So we did not win the prize and we did lose the job, or the lover, or good health. All those setbacks represent changes in life. The old friend stands for constancy, not changelessness.

I suppose it is blasphemous to think of God as the model of the "old friend," because it seems foolish to speak about God apart from the sacred, the Wholly Other. Why give the name *God* to that which we can take captive and reduce to chumminess? Still, we can talk about similes or likenesses between some ways of experiencing God and some ways of knowing humans.

Let's consider that in God there is great constancy united with loving flexibility. In theological circles the suggestion that God changes will raise heated arguments. Those who say God can and must change are led by the claims of a school of thought called "process theology." The process thinkers tell us that we have inherited bad answers about the nature of

God from earlier days in Christian life because we posed bad questions. They make their case in part to match the world of science and evolving life. All around us, in every aspect of a spinning and expanding universe, is motion and change. How can we hold on to a picture of God dominated by words like *all-powerful* and *all-encompassing?* Don't these demanding superlatives paint a portrait which cramps God in the notion that he cannot evolve or expand with the universe? And how can *can't* belong to our picture of an all-powerful God? The process thinkers insist that change is a part of God's nature.

Traditional theology likes to talk about the changelessness of God. It does so because it is rooted in a philosophy that forced such talk on believers. The philosopher quite naturally said that we should reserve the word *God* only for that which is Wholly Other posed against an imperfect world. That meant we had to begin by thinking of God as perfect. If we think of God as perfect, then any change in Godness or Godhead or God experience would seem to imply change from perfect to less perfect, and thus to imperfect. And *imperfect* has to mean less than God, or other than God. So the learned scholastics wrote books and libraries about God's aseity, God's being off there apart from what is created and exists. Most of all, the sages were taken up with changelessness, the human way of protecting the perfection of God.

Admittedly, the language about God not changing has its own power and in some contexts we do not need to throw it away. T. S. Eliot wrote about a "still point in a turning world," and there are ways we need access to God as axis when all around us changes. But the Christian God is a God of action, and action implies change.

God creates. Have you ever created without changing things—and yourself? Aren't you part of that garden, that meal, that poem? Perhaps God in a great act of creation overcomes the silence and the distance and changes, is changed. That is one dimension of the divine simile in friendship. We do not create friends, we locate them. But having recognized them, we create what was not there before: a bond, one that exacts commitment.

God experiences the fall of humans. Let people argue over what fallenness means, they will not find evidence that nothing has occurred to limit them, to make them less than perfect. So in response to the fall, God changes his relation to people. This is a second dimension of the divine simile embodied more in the old friend than in the new. Perhaps an old friend sets terms which you cannot meet; if there is to remain a bond, something has to give. You must recognize your limits and by gesture or voice point out the problem. A lot of good that does, unless the friend cherishes the ties enough to do some repenting or changing too. But a caring friend does not write you off, slam the door, break the connection.

God rescues. The story of fallenness is not the last chapter. In the Christian story, God visits that fallen human race in the man Jesus Christ. His cross and new life are not only symbols, they are points of enactment of a new relation with God. Without ever knowing quite what it means, believers have talked about this experience as being rescued or being saved. However we wish to conceive of Jesus—as related to God or as *an* expression or *the* expression of God—and however aware we are that language breaks down in such a discussion, we know that his very birth is a sign of changed relation in God, to God.

We are, of course, at the point of the breaking up of our simile between the divine life and the human when discussing this saving act. We have insisted with biblical writers that God creates the objects of love instead of locating them, which is just the opposite of friendship. So the friend cannot in the final sense rescue you. *But:* The old friend is often a vivid transmitter of the word and life of rescue and grace. I have known people who walked from church a thousand times having heard a word of grace, but having seen no evidence of it because there were no accepting people. They had no "old friends" who could support a word of forgiveness with a life of new relation.

So even at this delicate point, the old friend has some glimmers of simile to the divine. It is often the old friend who serves as a kind of priest at three in the morning, when we need someone to say, "God forgives you" or "I forgive you." This does not make the friend into the one who credentials forgiveness, if that image makes sense. That is, the friend is not the finally offended one, even if you have bruised her. But the friend sees to it that the word of grace finds embodiment. A particular human, a member of the human race who is important to you, stands for the whole human race when you need reacceptance.

God induces growth. Being saved is not the creation of finished products. Biblical language talks about nurture, maturing, "growing in grace." And the old friend offers a checkpoint for such growth. The last thing you want is to have a friend who will haunt you with a progress chart or a report card. But with a raised eyebow and a whispered "Let's go to lunch and talk about it," the old friend helps you measure gains and losses in the life of growth. In the case of God we speak of the Holy Spirit as the empowerer of growth. And the Holy Spirit touches the human spirit through certain kinds of old friends.

Not all friends fill these bills. Some of them hang on to oldness, and will not allow for the creation of anything new in our mutual relation. Many will not let us repent; they consider themselves friends by keeping mental records of old scores to settle. Not a few find it hard to be the representatives of a human race in which forgiving has to go on. And finally, some stand in the way of growth because they are corrupt and they want you to share their corruption. Maybe in the economy of friendship there has to be room for such wastage; such old friends need *you*, if you can risk creating, repenting, forgiving, and growing.

For now our point has to do with God and not with the degree to which old friends measure to the point of simile. We began by asking why we needed pictures of divine change. This does not lead to the notion that God is nothing but flux and represents nothing but adapting to our revisions. Likewise, our concern is not with a God who would please Plato and the philosophers by not changing. The point is that God is constant in the midst of change. You count on God. God embodies and expresses steadfast and enduring love.

And that is what old friends are. Changing, but constant. They create and grow with us, and we both experience changes in the chemistry between us with the passing of the years. But we can count on them.

There must be new friends as well. The new friendships, they say, cannot be as deep as the old ones. How could they be, since only old ones can have common roots in the origins of our lives and development? But new friendships can be animating and intense. We have seen this in retirement communities. An older couple or, better, an older single, usually widowed, pulls up roots and moves to a new community far from relatives and old friends. Climate beckons, or opportunity, or the desire to be with older people. Sometimes the move is pathetic, born of a desire to forget at a time when remembering should matter, born of a dream to gain new friends because one is unsuccessful with old ones. We cannot read all the motives, yet we can see integrity in the move.

Then, in the midst of the loneliness that afflicts one after the bags are unpacked but before the curtains and drapes are in place, comes a surprise. The new friends meet over cards, or at the restaurant, and possibly at church. "Why don't you come on over; let's get acquainted!" What does that person see in me with my puffing manner on the stairwell, the sag in my waistline or bustline? Yet I find myself included and, more surprising, I find the new friend accepting my reciprocal invitations and being open to my ideas.

The college dorm represents a hell of loneliness to the young person who does not consider herself good at making friends. But the accident of roommate assignment, often something to be endured in the roulette of human relations, now and then produces a new friend. The shy student cannot fake being "booked up," something she did as a high school senior. Her roommate can observe the schedule, and knows when hours in the library are necessary for study and when they are refuges from relations or signs of addiction to loneliness by someone who lives inside herself. So the new friend arranges for ways to take walks or go to parties, to test other friendships together. Soon the newly accepted one sees everything through the other's eyes, enough that both can compare. And she finds that the other needed a new friend as well. This is not to be a relation of your dependency, the collegian finds, but of something mutual.

As new friendships open, there is quite naturally some exploration and examination. "Dear Dad: I get along well with the roommate. She's really friendly. Of course, I am going to be careful, since I've been used before. And she might just be working out her Big Sister Ego on me. But so far as I can tell . . ." That is understandable language of caution. The student has been burned before. But if she transfers her cautions to the relation and does not move beyond the tentative and exploratory, the friendship stands no chance. If the unexamined life is not worth living, the over-examined life is not living at all.

New friendships enter our lives not as spontaneous divine love does, but seeking measures of equality. Yet here as so often the simile of divine relations plays a part. God has been known to stimulate wonder, work surprise, cause self-examination, and make all things new. So do the eyes borrowed from a new friend.

7

Friends and Relations

Being in love and being friends are not the only two alternatives for people·who are or wish to be in relation. After all, bitter enemies have some sort of engagement with each other, even if it is across the trenches or around the water cooler at the office. People who are friends play many additional roles in life. They can be involved with others as customers or sellers, employers or employees, dominators or victims. But among all the possibilities, the most confusing are those that force us to distinguish or define friendship in two kinds of connections—family relations and sexual relations.

One of the social forms that colors our way of being friends is the family, and no one can successfully or entirely sort out familial from friendly ties. Some adults crave friendship as compensation for wounds left from an early home life that gave them no security. Others find it difficult to express friendly ties because of these wounds; they never do learn to trust anyone else and to risk affection. On the other hand, many people are able to transform the warm family bonds of their childhood years into artful ways of relating to people as friends.

Because the family stamps so much of the personality, the family context does help determine the patterns of friendship its members will develop. For example, a young person entering the teens gradually becomes aware that his or her family's friends differ from the friends of another family. The neighbor's parents trek into the city each week or invite trekkers to their home for friendship's sake. One hears the sound of polkas, smells garlic, hears dancing, and knows that until late on Saturday night there will be boisterous sounds, punctuated in some seasons by the clatter of broken glass when someone who is too exuberant throws something. Yet my own parents, the teenager finds, hang out with very sedate friends who have difficulty loosening up. At airports there is a handshake but no embrace, and the conversation remains serious. One set of friends is churchgoing and another pagan; one close, the other, loose.

Thus, the family takes on some responsibility for shaping children so that they can express the life of being friends. The family that has been so loose or disconnected that it never becomes a center of morale may drive its members to seek friendship but will seldom equip them for it. At the opposite extreme, parents who are too tight and protective may fabricate webs and entanglements that children cannot escape. When the kids finish high school they should go off to find friends, but the family

closes in and keeps setting the terms for all relations. Any time the children spend with friends is only grudgingly yielded by the parents. When the children come home from college or from their own homes, they are not set free to sustain the weak ties of friendship that the family permitted earlier. They are subjected to a suffocating embrace. Brothers and sisters keep score of the time they spend away from mother and dad. The new generation gets no space for itself, and friends by their very attractiveness inspire guilt.

The home that is secure need not induce claustrophobia. If it serves as a magnet for building morale, then friends will represent the first stage of a child's socializing in the larger world. School is more neutral; the sphere of jobs can be perplexing; the big outside word is probably hostile. Friends give a child the first confidence that he or she can act beyond the family circle and survive.

Being married also colors every aspect of friendship. In the biblical notion—one that is often forgotten even in religious marriage manuals—something new occurs in individuals entering a marriage. It is not that two people who have become friends wanted to transform their friendship into love and love into marriage. Nor is it that two solitudes found each other in passion and, in order to stabilize their emotions, made a commitment that was supposed to last through the years and to legitimate the way they express that passion. Most certainly it is not just a legal contract, off there in the record books with the dog licenses and the windshield stickers, waiting to be broken some day.

In marriage people become bonded; the two, in biblical language, are "one flesh." The marital vows in a sense change the way the universe holds together for a wedded couple. In the Catholic tradition, therefore, marriage is a sacrament, a holy bonding, and not an arrangement based on companionship. And once two people have made their vows and become one flesh, their other relations in life also change character.

In some respects, being married places restrictions on the ways a person can be a friend. In the modern world, it is becoming increasingly common for both spouses to work, and thus they may have very little leisure time to spend with each other. If they nourish strong friendships apart from each other, he obsessively going fishing with his pals as she just as fanatically hangs out with old friends, they will put a strain on their marriage. If one spouse has an exclusive friend of the opposite sex there will quite naturally be tension. And even a circle of friends can induce jealousy. "Wedding bells are breaking up that old gang of mine" is a line in a song, but not always a reality. If the old gang persists, *it* can break up a marriage. Finding ways to include both spouses' friends in the couple's activities and even to blend two circles of friendship is a demanding art in many a marriage.

Having noted potential difficulties, however, we must note that friends, including two pooled clusters of friends, more often add to marriage. If we observe that two people are "all wrapped up in each other," the words may be intended as a comment about a quality of the couple's love—but they are likely to be a judgment on two selfish souls. Wrapped up in each other, the pair is closed off, and their mutual absorp-tion may be nothing more than an expression of two selfishnesses. Two possessive people, they clutch each other because they demand total devotion and cannot risk being unnoticed for five minutes.

For the married couple, then, the reality of friends is as much a means of access to the larger world as it is for the child breaking out of the parental cocoon. Being open to friends breaks exclusiveness so that married people can rejoin the human race and be of service to others. Having friends and giving friend-ship room to grow alongside the primary relation of marriage is not as demanding as warding off the enemies of married life or of a specific couple. Thus, a couple's friendships provide a good training ground for the struggle with the surrounding world. But to talk in these terms makes everything sound programmatic. Friends belong also to the sheer enjoyment of marriage in this bleak era for wedded life.

Is the bond between parents and children to go by the name of friendship? Those who fear such a blurring of categories often bring two sets of con-cerns to the issue. First, they want mother love to be suffocatingly rich, allowing none of the breathing space that friendship provides. Friendship is re-served for children down the block in the case of the young, and for old college roommates among the old folks. Children are supposed to be given over to an exclusive devotion to their parents; in turn, a father who reaches out to his child in friendship risks cooling the parental tie. Second, such people fear sentimentalization of family ties. If parents and children become pals and use the word *friendship* to describe their relation, where is the needed distance between them? Do not parents need to remain partly aloof for the sake of authority? If they become pals to their children, how do they invoke the status that comes with their roles? How do they preserve family order?

Perhaps the whole issue has to do with quibbling over the word *friendship* and what it means. Parent-child relations vary so radically, depending upon whose house we are thinking about, that it is hard to be prescriptive about names for them or limiting about varieties of bonds. In every developing family, there are constant subtle adjustments between the old and the young. One day the parents fear that they have been too severe, so they tilt toward leniency. The next day they fear that they will be tainted with the brush that spells Permissive, so they gently twist the knobs that regulate family ties until they can thunder at the children.

If their shuttling between extremes allows them no stops along the way at points which others call friendship, both generations deprive themselves. Parents who make exhausting demands for the affection of their children have not learned that a family is not exclusive or permanent. A couple comes onstage; they are to reveal the family as an art form. It is not an art like architecture or painting, finished and there for the ages. Their art is like the ballet, to be danced when the curtain goes up and the stage lights on. Soon the footlights will dim, the house lights will go up, the curtain will fall. The dance is over and the dancers move on, with memories, snapshots, and other stages ahead. Parents who do not learn how to let go, to anticipate saying good-bye, are doing a disservice to family relations. But if parents and children are friends, they will have been learning how to bid good-byes. Friendly good-byes are forms of practicing for death, but they temper the bleak prospect by their distance from tragedy.

If parents do nothing to call forth response from their children, there is no danger that they will become friends. They may share the same roof. Once a week between junk food stops or sandwiches left on the kitchen counter they may sit across from each other at mealtime, if not in a true meal. For the rest, the kids are farmed out to Little League and Girl Scouts and the parents turn the television dials or go off to their club. They are finding no common basis for morale, no central theme for their stories. They are inadvertently practicing for the day when both generations will complain that they have fallen out of communication, whereas they had never fallen into it.

Friendship, then, is not the only name and what it points to is not the only relation possible between healthy parents and children. But if they are never tempted to give that name to their bond, and never tempted even to aspire to friendship of sorts, something is missing. One way to build friendship between relatives is to enlarge the zone called *family*. In the modern world, we are often cut off from the clan or the tribe. That is, no mixture of elders can pass on signals to the young or pick up new ones from them. Whereas uncles and aunts once lived in blurred closeness to their nieces and nephews, today's large firms or military agencies often call their personnel to move. This frequently prevents people from forming ties to relatives outside their immediate families who may live thousands of miles away.

Perhaps when the clan and the tribe were strong there was less opportunity or necessity for parents and children to be friends. Other relatives filled the role. Today, with two parents and two children (and sometimes a psychiatrist) making up what we call the nuclear family, new pressures have developed. If family members are not friends, their relationships will display destructive patterns of authority or anarchy. If they are each other's only familial-type friends, their expectations of one another must be too high. The parents dare not fail in any day's relations, and the children have to prove themselves with no room for testing and experimenting against restraint. As most mothers enter the work force outside the home, the continuity they once provided for their children is broken. For some, this has meant that the family is no longer a center of morale and has become only destructive, something to be outlived.

What we are beginning to see among thoughtful people is a pattern, sometimes official and sometimes unofficial, of what I call collegial families. They make up a collegium, a college; they are colleagues. In the case of my own family—we are Christians who baptize our children with godparents taking part—the nucleus of the collegial group tends to be parents of our godchildren and our children's godparents. But the club is not so exclusive, nor, ideally, should it be made up of people who have complete sympathy of outlook or background.

Collegial families quietly and sometimes even formally covenant together. Many of us bought camping space or cabin plots on an island together, and in summers we can test and extend the larger family bonds of friendship. The children in our group do not always have to "make it" with mother and father; there is always an unrelated (by blood) uncle or aunt down the block or across the metropolis who can perhaps respond better than anyone with whom the youngster shares one suffocating roof. Decisions about purchases, colleges, commitments—all of these get talked about in the collegial circle. If one set of parents loses perspective, their friends can set things right without making a noisy production of their correction. If someone feels beleaguered or bereft, a friend confirms him or her. Children who have the good fortune to grow up in such circumstances find that their parents are not eccentrics simply because they try to embody or impart values the rest of society does not cherish. Something of their world finds echoes in that of unrelated uncles, aunts, and cousins.

Friendship finds reinforcement in traditions. Again, the nuclear family of four people has a hard time sustaining them. But collegial families have a better chance. In our own case, for years we were called upon to join another family during Christmas week for a pizza supper in a borrowed high-rise apartment. From there we were off to entertainment at Second City, a club featuring comic improvisations and skits we all enjoyed. These collegial relatives took pains to be home and to clear this special night for the reinforcement of friendships that might suffer neglect when New Year's dispersal came. Another example: Each year we have foregone the traditional, Norman Rockwell-style kind of family Thanksgiving dinner for the cause of a trek to visit

175

members of our collegial family. We have counted three generations of this family among our friends, although only two remain. Together we celebrate the season, ponder the passing of the year, project plans for a new generation. No archaic people were more bound to myth and ritual than are we, as are any who take pains to turn the friendship circle into an expanded family.

Friendship is not the same in every age and every culture, and change in the world around us forces people to reappraise what it means to be a friend. Nothing has brought more change in our own culture, at least to half the human race, than has the growth of women's consciousness of what it is to be women. As recently as several decades ago, friendship tended to be the chief tie open to unmarried women, as if it were a consolation prize for the wedding they never achieved. And among the married, women's friendships tended to be either restricted to the circle approved by the couple or viewed as temporary escapes from a constrictive marriage. The husband was unfeeling, so the wife could take refuge in long morning phone calls to her old friend down the block.

As the number of women in the work force increases, opportunities for women to make friends on their own in new ways have multiplied as well. The need to achieve new legal status and make their presence felt called for the establishment of a women's movement. While many of the ties between sisters in the movement have been pragmatic, or intoxicating as partnership in any revolution can be, friendships that are not merely functional or ideological have also developed. In the act of finding other freedoms, women found new freedoms to discover friends and cultivate friendships. And as together they explored the roots of womanhood in religion, history, and literature, many of them enjoyed their mutual search. They found new friendships as they pored over texts or worked through libraries or Bibles reworking the profound symbols of life.

In the process, women began to detect that, just as men in groups bond distinctively, so do women. Observers might well argue about what characteristics are distinctly relevant to women's friendships. I once attempted to collate some of these themes and found them maddeningly contradictory. Some women argued that friendships between women always had to be cramped and nervous because men were there to limit them. Others felt that as friends, women are the really free gender, since they are not as competitive as men. They argued that men use friendship as part of their game of succeeding. It is too soon to be able to present many scientific findings on women and friendship. But that women are finding it important to cherish friendship and to see it in a new light is obvious; their attention will yield riches as years pass.

As far as men are concerned, friendly relations are changing in part because of the response and sometimes reaction to the women's movement. Even men who resist the feminization of their clubs have benefited from a new freedom to express themselves more openly and with more variety as friends of other men. Among the reasons for this is what someone has called "the somatic revolution," which has changed the way that people in Western culture think of their bodies and themselves.

The somatic revolution cultivates a sense of the body. We are present to each other as bodies, say the philosophers of the phenomenological school. We are not spirits trapped in bodies as the Greeks often thought; we are not souls trying to be sprung free from the prison of bodily presence. The Hebrews had it more nearly right: We are ensouled bodies, who make ourselves present to each other as irreplaceably distinct bodily beings. Wider acceptance of this view has brought a decline of shame over the body, a change readily exploited by cologne manufacturers and hairdressers. The new understanding has had more positive effects. In the past, for example, convention did not allow men to touch one another. One could place a hand on the shoulder of someone in need, but this was a highly ritualized and formal gesture, and the hand had to be withdrawn as soon as the crisis passed. For men, a slap on the back seemed more appropriate. It kept the distance needed for competing.

Yet men do not relate solely through competition. The encouraging pat that one football hulk imparts to another during a televised game seen by millions may be partially motivated by a team spirit that arises from dreams of trophies and higher salaries. But more often it is a genuine and friendly outreach of the sort that has helped legitimate more tender, more informal bonds among men *not* dressed as gladiators for combat. Cultural habits die slowly, and a man may not yet be encouraged to weep in front of friends, or to bury his head on the shoulder of another. Zorba the Greek pioneered a new expression of exuberance for the masses in solitary male dance or with a circle of males. But he is a less lonely figure in the generation that came after him than in the one that went before.

As women move into positions of power, it is possible that they will acquire many of the problems of friendship that men have known. Many of these are webbed into the issue of power itself. Within a firm, the male management traditionally did not allow for friendship because the corporation forced competition on all. How dared one let his guard down, and possibly become vulnerable to a co-worker who might trample a rival on the way up? Other friendships tended to follow the lines of vocation and caste. Assistant Expediters In Charge Of, or whatever they are called, played golf with Assistant Expediters In Charge Of, or their equivalents, at another firm. This meant that any time spent off the course, in the locker room, or over drinks had to be full of banter and guarded language lest one give away secrets or make openings that competitors could exploit. In this late stage of business civilization such obstacles to male friendship seem only to grow, and women entering the work force take them on. Service professions in which practitioners are not so visibly in competition with each other dwindle in number. Meanwhile, more and more young adults line up for the Master of Business Administration degree, carrying away with it no rationale except the values of free enterprise competition.

Having friends and being friends will not turn the culture around by themselves or transform business

179

relations so that they follow less competitive styles. But people who put a premium on the life of friends can ward off some of the worst. If they do not reverse all trends, at least they have taken a stand and been witnesses for values other than those that predominate in a business culture. We are not likely to replace that culture unless there be a total collapse of the economy. Besides, all alternatives carry their own threats: We have already spoken of the difficulty of being friends in the context of ideology, including that of the political and economic left. A different question must preoccupy us now. We need not concentrate all our energies on the question "What should replace a business civilization?" Instead it is better to ask, "Is a humane business civilization possible?" And, if so, "How do we attain it?" Answers to that question are certain to accent the role of the friend as a softener of hard relations. The friend by his or her very existence is a judgement on the over-programmed life. Until we find alternatives to the "laws of the jungle" by which we presently organize life and set the terms for the professions, we can subvert some of the claims of the old order. That means withholding some consent from those who would compute out such inefficiencies as friends. More positively, being subversive means cherishing friends even if they do not fit into the scheme of the corporation, the university, or whatever else demands our soul and all its hours.

Now at this point, I confess to having cheated a bit. In preparing these pages, I consulted not only those parts of the library where the giants Aristotle, Augustine, and Aquinas speak up out of silence across the ages. I checked to see what is in the contemporary literature as well, to find what people in our time consider to be urgent topics. What dared I not leave out? What would I have forgotten?

The worry most consistently voiced by the advice-givers concerns the possibility of friendship's transformation into sexual expression. Perhaps if I were writing at half my age that concern would have been on page one. Perhaps when I am twice my age, I will deem it worthy of only half the meager space it receives here. May it never disappear. But frankly, it did not at first occur to me that these hazards demanded such bold treatment. Cannot a happy marriage satisfy some dimensions of life so fully that no temptation threatens? Not likely. We are too familiar with the stories of people who were secure, or thought they were, and then were lured away by new attractions. Could it be that infidelity occurs only in lives that have a void, just as alcoholics and junkies, it is said, fill a similar emptiness with their addictions? If this were true, we could not explain lapses from fidelity in people whose lives seem full, but who nevertheless become the lovers of people who were their friends.

So we face up to the issue. Which is an awfully grim way to start. Better to begin off-balance and playfully. Why worry? If we think of friendships that move to heterosexual love among people who are not married, only the usual moral and ethical norms come into play, the questions that arise when people fall in love apart from friendship. Of course, moving to "being in love" from "being friends" is a change; in one sense, we could say that erotic love has meant the end of many a friendship. But on its more positive side, we might smile wisely and say that friendship has been known to survive among lovers, and we have known a number of married couples who were also friends. Or who began by being friends.

So far as friends who are not of the same sex are concerned, when one of them is married to someone else the risks are higher. Here there cannot be a movement toward erotic love between friends without a threat to fidelity. Because these hazards are there, we often hear the counsel that one must remain impersonal and distant, friendless and unfriendly across the bar of the sexes. But this might very well do nothing more than make the lures seem greater, put a golden apple out of reach, suggest greener grass beyond the bonds of fidelity. Besides, the records are reasonably full of infidelities that occur between partners in an affair who are not now, never have been, and are not in danger of becoming friends. They may merely use each other. Thus, avoiding friendships is not a way of removing temptations.

An evidence of the way friendships with members of the opposite sex sustain themselves harmlessly, indeed creatively, through the decades, will spring to the mind of anyone who knows older people who have been widowed. On this day as I write the mail brings me a card: "Margaret M. and Robert R. are happy to announce their marriage. . . ." Robert, old friend, example to my children, raconteur, a buoyant man, remarrying! What happened to his wife? Have we lost track of her so totally? And inside is the hand-written note: "Since losing our dear Betty, Margaret and I were two very lonely people. Then we realized we needed and lovèd each other and this is the happy result." We dissect those lines as we would a verse of Scripture. Margaret and Robert were not merely "lonely people." They were people of rich and full lives, now temporarily saddened. "Then we realized . . . we loved each other." They had been close for years, and were certainly friends. But Robert's marriage to Betty did not permit a second thought of the sort that has now developed and bloomed.

Many a happy marriage has been solemnized between longtime friends after mutual widowing left them both solitary. Through years of friendship they had already passed crises together, shared vacations together with their spouses, made decisions together. It would have surprised any of the four to have had their friendship disrupted years before even by the question of exclusive and erotic love between the unmarried partners. Yet after the death of one partner in each couple, love between the survivors grew naturally. The latency for this special kind of commitment and for sexual attraction must have been there through the earlier years, but it occured to no one to give it expression or to quicken suspicion by bringing up the topic. Maybe that all goes under the word *sublimation*, but that does not make it unnatural or bad. For the sake of our loves and marriages we may do a lot of sublimating, without grudge and as a grace. And to avoid friendship out of fear of sex would be to overendow sex with meaning and terror, and to deprive life of subtler expressions.

Of course, married men and women who have close friends of the opposite sex must be thoughtful and take special measures. Cultivating these friend-

184

ships mutually is the best protection for a couple, for time spent with such a friend is then public, and the hint of the clandestine diminishes. Being sure to tell the spouse of encounters and feelings can help the cause. Taking care not to nurture the friendship in settings conducive to sexual expression is quite obviously a sensible safeguard.

Rather than point to the risks, however, it makes as much sense to urge a very large circle of friends and a reasonable sphere of close friends across the lines of gender on almost anyone. Such ties lead to a development of the arts of friendship, and these full-time preoccupations are demanding of other resources than those claimed by love, including erotic love. To make an analogy, perfecting the art of Sunday painting may distract me from learning to play the guitar well enough for it to become pleasurable. But my life is rather full without guitar. If I am good at neither, my life may have a vacuum, a barren space, which almost any kind of excitement can then fill.

In any discussion of friendships between adults of the same sex, people find that they must tread cautiously near the edges of the subject of homosexuality. If two women friends share an apartment, socialize together, and have much in common, those at a distance presume that they are not friends but lovers, and that their relations are also sexual. What one has to say about such whisperings—for they almost always come undertoned—depends much on one's attitudes toward homosexuality itself. That subject is draped in enough mystery that we cannot pretend to settle or even address it in a short space while keeping a long eye on friendship. To produce intelligent comment would be to commit ourselves to kinds of medical and psychiatric research, theological or sociological positions, that are beyond our present range.

To make that point, picture the different responses that would be evoked by the information that "Anna and Anne are lesbian" when heard among a circle of lesbians on one hand and at an anti-gay-rights forum on the other. If the listeners feel that homosexuality is all right, then seeing friends of the same sex as expressive lovers is fine. If it is to be abhorred, then the love that dare not speak its name is spoken, and possibilities for free friendship are blighted. Most of us find ourselves somewhere between those camps, somewhat freed from the investment both of them have in their commitment, yet partly threatened by both camps to make a commitment.

In the ground between the extremes, there are some things that bear saying. One can minimize the issue simply on statistical grounds. In almost any community, the number of people who "on the average" are expressing homosexual tendencies or living out such a commitment will not match the number of very good friends of the same sex. So we begin by presuming that the vast majority of such intimate bondings do not issue in sexual expression.

Second, statistics aside, we can take the pressure off by recognizing that all kinds of human relations have dimensions of sexuality attached to them. Sex is not a part of life confined to a night a week or a place below the belt; rather, it subtly infuses bodily presence and spiritual being. Followers vote for leaders who have sex appeal; attractive people cannot help making use of that appeal in dealing with others. The veil over the virgin does not make her an

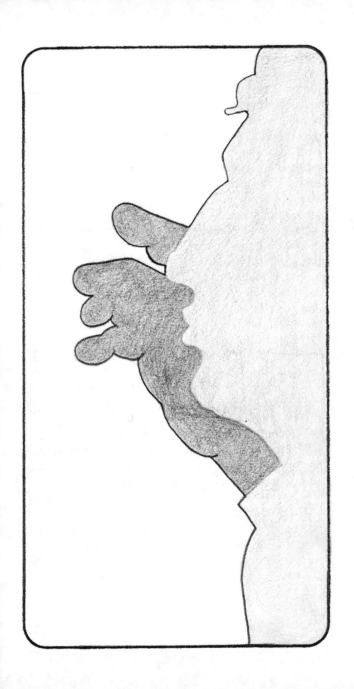

asexual being, and the cassock of a celibate has never yet been known to shroud the sexual being of a perfectly chaste priest. Even the most innocent extramarital connections on the part of happily married monogamists retain a trace of the sexual: a wink, a pat, a fond look, a tone of voice, a partner held while dancing. That each of these could be transformed into something that violates the bonds of fidelity is as clear as that their sexual dimension is unavoidable and that life would be terribly poorer if they were ignored or blotted out.

So it is with same-sex friends. Homosexual tendencies may be far from the front our minds, repressed if they exist at all. And yet bodies send out signals. To deny friendship because of this factor, or to refuse to be close to another human being because there might be a sexual nuance to the relation seems the height of folly.

One benefit among the mixed boons and banes of homosexual expression's increased visibility and acceptability in modern culture is this: No longer can a whisper condemn or a hint destroy. Once upon a time, even people innocent of homosexual expression had to be so discreet they seemed obsessed with keeping a distance. Today, when ravenously heterosexual football players pat each other's rumps, it has become safer for milder souls to put their arms around each other without being consigned to a sexual category other than the one that they inhabit.

Along with that wider acceptability comes another possibility: the courage to say, "none of your business." I have long cherished the little symbol of an old San Francisco restaurant in the form of a coin the management gave out. Under the profile of a rather happy—one would once have say *gay*—Irish character, was the line, "It's my life. I live it. I love it. Criticism be damned." That is not a base for all kinds of relations in a world in which we are members one of another and where our solitudes must connect. But it is good self-therapy for the people who wonder, "Do I dare?"

A final word on the possibility of confusing friendship with homosexual love: While the chance of crossing a line unsought is always there, the hazard is no greater than is that of crossing a similar line heterosexually. In fact, temptations are more frequent in the second case, since more of the world is heterosexual. But if one so respected or, in this translation, was so terrified by, the power of sexuality that it had to blight all other ties, then happily married couples would have to avoid frequent and intimate company with other couples lest there be a confusion of attractions among spouses. The temptations are obvious—they have made up the plots of a million broken marriages and as many bad novels. That there are safeguards against transgression among people of will who prize fidelity is more obvious in the tens of millions of unbroken marriages and the plots of a few good novels. For the fearful, a spread of friendships and a range of varying commitments to different kinds of friends may be among the better protections against making sexual commitments that in saner moments we would not choose.

8

Friendship Tested

People who resist having friends take on one set of problems. Loneliness and isolation gnaw at those who are incapable of being friends or being befriended. It would be nice to picture friendship as the arrival of a utopia in which all turned out well—though that kind of niceness might also induce a killing boredom.

But people who do have friends take on another set of problems. They have egos that collide with other egos, wills that clash with other wills. Their drives will not always match the desires of others within their circles of friendship. They do not stop being agents of conflict simply because they have friends. Anger is in their arsenal of emotions, and it will find its way of jeopardizing friendly relations. One partner may make unreasonable demands on the other, or spend too much time chewing an ear and expecting counsel. We do friendship a disservice if we overlook these problems. One way to address them is to begin by throwing the issues against a big enough screen that we can see them clearly. In this case we will again use the simile of divine relations to human connections.

I once heard a curious phrase about the love of God. According to the writer, divine love may take the form of a *zornige Liebe*, a "wrathful love." In this as in all attempts to deal with the strangeness of the divine, the phrase-maker had to settle for an inadequate expression. Of course, we assume that we know how to separate anger from love. When I am angry, either something has gone wrong in me to jeopardize my love and lovability, or something is wrong in you, my friend, and I need the strongest sort of emotion to tell you off or keep you at a distance. When I am loving, I cannot be angry. And when I am caring, in the way that friends can be, I must suppress my standards and let you do as you please, without letting anything bother me.

Elegantly simple, perhaps, but not true—at least not so easily. The writer's attempt to speak of the extremes in God within one phrase falls short of the divine reality, but it points to something of which we are somehow aware. In biblical faith God is so different from us, and the sacred so remote from our profane feet, that when we violate perfection, God—in this picture drawn from human emotions—is wrathful. It is intrinsic in the nature of God to show anger toward that which violates the good. Some of the biblical pictures are so curiously patterned after human action that God comes off looking like a petty tyrant. But most of the time anyone who thinks deeply about it sees reasons for the anger of the Holy.

Such wrath would drive us away from, not *to* God, were it not for the fact that under it all, or prior to it, we have sensed that God "is" love. God accepts us when we are outside the range of acceptance. Because we have heard that this is the nature of God, and because we have checked it out, we pay attention when the wrathful side of God is revealed. It does not break our tie with the divine.

On an infinitely more domestic and graspable scale, something like this wrathful love can touch humans during the course of a fulfilling friendship. You would not call another person *friend* did she not possess qualities that you admire. You count on the friend for affection and for friendship's kind of love. But because the two of you are close, you will disappoint your friend more than will someone at a distance. A thousand times she will explain what course of action pleases her most, and each time you are neglectful. Finally your friend "lets off steam." But among friends, being angry is often a more creative emotion than feeling hurt. If we have learned the limits of anger and have found rites for overcoming it, expression of such feelings can clear the air.

Of course, if we bring nothing but temper and irritation to our relationship, the friend may drift away. She has no reason at all to "take it" or to care about its source *unless* that source is a person liked or loved, important in life. By finding rites for overcoming anger, I mean that we find ways to ensure that it will not have the field to itself. We know how far to go and when to stop. We are not so egotistical as to think that we have a right to dominate our relation to a friend by setting all standards and absorbing all disappointments. Maybe our friend has a right to a bit of "wrathful friendliness" too, to even the score. By speaking of the rites of anger, I also refer to the fact that creative people can devise means of conversing about the strong emotions that occasionally should erupt between friends.

In the end, anger in the context of friendship plays its part in the economy of emotions between people who know each other well. Now and then we hear tragic stories of friends who fell out to the point that disappointment led to outrage and outrage to murder. We are less likely to hear of the channels through which people vent their emotions in ways that will not disrupt the world, channels that can soon again be passages for caring. Friends have more motives for ending anger than continuing it; their friendship constitutes a better basis for building on trying experiences than for letting them shatter relations. The same is not true when anger erupts between people who have no previous shared history. Wrathful love has built-in controls. Loving love is sloppy. Wrathful wrath kills. The combination, a curious joining of anger and friendly love, offers alternatives in a world of hatreds.

Having friends is not a way of avoiding conflict in life; rather, it impels people to find ways to make conflict creative. Some years ago people used to play a game about cloning. When it was believed that we were on the point of being able to change human nature or the makeup of the human race in the laboratory, speculators began to talk about the shape that new race should take. What might be done to alter the human makeup? How could humans be changed? What qualities should be screened out of them?

A common answer was that the experimenter would eliminate the element that induced conflict. Thus, if one were to duplicate parents in their cloned offspring while eugenically preventing "unscientific" births, screening out conflictual people would be an experimenter's most important concern. Then there would be no war, little violence, and little threat to safety. Utopia would be on the way. But no sooner had people written such a scenario than questions began to arise: If you eliminate conflict and all forms of competition, will you not eliminate creativity? Will not the human adventure end? It was impossible to resolve such questions, since the necessary experiments would cause unimaginable and irretrievable changes in all aspects of human life. Interestingly, the answers games-players gave usually told us much about their own values. Those who touted free enterprise competition protested most loudly. Those who believed in socialist cooperative life felt most ready to make the move.

The difficulty of cloning, and perhaps its permanent impossibility for humans, has led to less speculating of this sort in recent times. But enough has occurred already that thoughtful people tend to agree more than they had in the past that the impulse to be in conflict colors life. Whether this impulse is a trace of some particularly vicious strain humans inherited from simian ancestors or whether it is the worst blight of Original Sin, we seem to be stuck with it as a part of human nature. The trick is to channel it creatively into harmless outlets or to devise rites to control it. And in a world of conflict, being a friend or having a friend seems to be one of the best checks.

The problem is that for many people friendship only presents one more combat zone. Being friends and never coming into conflict is probably a sign of apathy; people who care deeply about anything in the world are going to disagree and, if they are free, to express their disagreement. If one friend were to dominate the other so that there could be no voicing of conflict their friendship would be jeopardized or might change its character until the relation no longer deserved the name *friendship*. Yet when friends dispute, they also risk losing each other. Fallen-out friends are central to the story of many a fallen empire of generations-long feuds.

Conflict raises an issue similar to the one we explored in our discussion of competition in a business civilization: Since we cannot do away with it, how do we make it creative; how do we see to it that a more humane circle of friendships emerges? If suppressing and avoiding it are not possible, the best alternative is to anticipate conflict and set up structures for handling it. By speaking openly about the potential problem or by devising little gestures and kidding routines, partners in friendship set up a circumstance for handling disagreements. They have in a way resolved not to let anything break their bond. They might conceive of their arguments or differences as scrimmages for the larger game of life. The coach who has the best interests of a player in mind does not keep him or her from the front lines during practice. Athletes need seasoning, not avoidance.

So in the scrimmages of friendship. If two people share a deep bond of like-mindedness or affection, it will survive debate and conflict. And precisely for this reason, friendship is one of the more congenial zones in which people can test the limits of argument. By not expecting serenity every day a friend avoids the dangers of boredom. By establishing rules and playing by them, the friend outlasts conflict just as he or she does on the squash court or after arm-wrestling. "It's only a game," however seriously we have to take it while it is in progress.

Friendship does represent lower risks than do other relations in which the partners are temporary adversaries. Lovers' quarrels might lead to sweet reunions, but first they will issue in torrents of words that neither partner ever forgets; they remain in memory and prospect to haunt a love. The intimacy imposed by marriage makes the stakes so high that serious conflict can lead to divorce. The family has enough societal sanction for inducing claustrophobia that conflict there—as between mothers and daughters in the kitchen or between fathers and sons over lifestyles—can blight a personality. There is no escape.

Friendship allows for less intimacy and more freedom. A person does not have to make things work quite so convincingly among friends as with a mate or a child. This means that somewhere in life there is a space between life-and-death combat on one hand and boredom or illusion on the other, a space where people can be true to themselves and their values even as they wrestle with another and with competing values at middle distance. Here as so often, friendship, written off as a "second-best" kind of relation (when compared to family, to love, to

organizations for justice), reveals the function it possesses but society overlooks.

Being a friend can mean being tested. Those who are sentimental about friendship have not interviewed enough people. They would be surprised to find how hard it is for many people to rejoice in the good fortune of their friends. One of the most disturbing features about the human heart, its tendency toward jealousy, leaped out at me once in a line by novelist Gore Vidal:

"Every time a friend succeeds, I die a little."

We are ready to hear, "Every time an enemy succeeds, I die a little." The people who link animal and human behavior, or the experts on the selfish gene who do not think true generosity exists, set us up to believe that friends hope only their enemies will have bad times. Why seek friends except for mutual defense and aggression against the foe? On those terms, it would be expedient to hang out only with the apes who can pull their weight, the avengers who have the muscle and courage to do in the outsider who threatens. Any weakness or failure in the band of allies could jeopardize security and life itself.

Flip that over, then: Whatever strengthens the muscle or morale of a friend is to my benefit. Not so, says Gore Vidal, whose blurted confession, some tell me, matches something they have felt all along. I do not know how widespread this emotion is. But after I thought about it, examples started coming to mind. Some years ago I won an award, what looked like an earning but felt like a grace. From all over the country there came letters of greeting, spontaneous bursts that can make one's day or one's life. We are glad for you, dear friend, most of them said. They did not sound as if they wanted me to share the prize with them; I did not suspect them of being friendly now so that I could speak up for them when they were in the running. Other letters were just a tinge more grudging. Not bad, old boy; of course, there were more deserving ones in the running, but the judges were specialists in your field. I join you in being thankful for good luck. What are the reasons for such a response?

Experts on the mind know little about the roots of jealousy and envy, and we do not have to tug at those roots now. For the moment the point we must stress is the testing that friendship brings. One of the ways to enter the human race, to be ready for encounters with enemies, is to have survived having friends. They make the first demands upon us and our emotions because they are close at hand.

Some time ago, a young lady of my acquaintance phoned in tears. As her tears abated, there was still quavering in her voice, and a touch of shuddering in her tone and outlook. Something had gone terribly wrong. As she quieted, she brought up the name of someone I knew to be her best friend. Had Norma, let's call her, been taken ill? How long had she to live? Was there an auto accident? Cancer? None of that. I breathed more easily. Was there, then, a misunderstanding, a falling out? Had one of them slammed the door in the other's face? Did they need a veteran arbitrator to thaw their frozen relations? All of that, said my friend, she could have coped with on her own.

What, then, was the problem? It turned out that there was a vacancy in their organization. Someone

had to move on or move up. My friend sounded as if she felt that she was next in line, ready to win the Most Qualified Candidate of the Year award. Good. She deserved it. Could she live with the disappointment if management had the bad sense to pass her up? Yes and no. Why yes? Because they might bring in someone from out of town, somewhere else in the firm. Then why a possible no? What could go wrong?

"They're also considering Norma. She could conceivably get it."

"So, wouldn't you be happy? Aren't you each other's best friend?"

"Yes, we are best friends, and no, I wouldn't be happy. *Because* we are best friends. We wouldn't be, then."

"Would Norma be over you, a bad boss?"

"No, she wouldn't be in the same line of staff, so that would be no problem. I just can't stand the idea of something good happening to a friend and not to me."

"You mean you'd rather have an unknown outsider or maybe even someone you don't like have good fortune, while you and Norma share lower rank?"

"I'm afraid that is what I would rather have. That's how I feel."

"Do you realize how weird this phone conversation would sound to anyone who doesn't know you but knows you claim to be Norma's friend?"

"Let it be weird, then. And we don't *claim* to be friends. We *are* friends. Our friendship has weathered everything except the success of one and the jealousy of the other. I'd rather not put it to that test."

Every time a friend succeeded, she died a little. Someone as close as a friend, someone whose more intimate thoughts we know, holds up a mirror to our emotions even when we do not want to look. When something good happens to a successful stranger, that is a remote story as if from another planet. We need pay no more attention to it than to a chart of the bureaucracy in a foreign land or a fictional film about an organization half a world away. But when something good happens up close, unless it directly benefits us it threatens us. My caller had not seen direct benefit to her in anything that enhanced Norma's life. She was more preoccupied with herself and her ego than with her bond to another human. So long as neither leaped forward with a success or a grace, they could live a happy and untested life together.

Lest the suspense that flows out of that phone call distracts from our larger plot, I should say that both Norma and her fearful friend advanced in their own lines and lived happily ever after. Or will until one of them succeeds again and the other, yet untested, dies a little. In cases such as these we must learn to view the friend as an agent of testing, a gift in the form of an obstacle, a revealer of our darker side whose challenge makes possible great growth—but never without struggle.

Alongside envy in friendships is another problem: insatiability. Some people can never get enough of the friend. They become dependent, selfish, even overwhelming in their ability to consume the time and emotions of a friend. True friends know that there are times when we ought to withhold marks of friendship for the good of others. But just as in the world of sex there may be people who evidently cannot satisfy themselves, as in the world of food there are gluttons, so in human relations some people seem to have an insatiable desire to use up the time of their friends until they use up their friends. They can never bear to be alone, fearing the terror of the night around them or the demons within. Obsessed, they have cut themselves off from casual contact with people. So those who have permitted themselves to become the friends of such people come now to be exploited. The phone rings at any hour: "What are you doing? Can you come over? We're getting a few fellows over to play cards. You can't? What kind of a friend are you?" And as the receiver falls, one hears a hurt. Next time the friend calls or sees you, he will do what he can to make you feel guilty, to take or keep you captive: You owe me more hours, he implies. You have no right to a life of your own.

Setting out to satisfy such an attitude is no more helpful than pouring drink down the throat of an alcoholic: The taste only grows. Most people find a natural rhythm in their friendships and locate quiet ways to pass on signals to others. We do have jobs, families, interests, and privacies that need protection from friends, and it is important to guard these zones and to signal when someone intrudes across their lines. If a subtle code does not successfully limit the friend's demands on us, we must make clear statements of our needs. And if a friendship cannot survive the setting of boundaries, we must question whether the relation ever was deep: Was the friend anything more than a consumer, eating up our time and affections? On the other hand, if we too readily draw the boundaries and allow for no sacrifice or inconvenience, then it may be as clear from the friend's point of view that no investment in friendship is forthcoming from us. Better to say good-bye, she may think, to look for other, better matches.

Friendship is a strenuous form of human activity. Most of us remember having had more friends as children than we have as adults, or at least we were conscious of our bonds meaning more to us then. No doubt that is because children are more free of care and thus freer to cultivate connections than are adults. And perhaps they are also more aware of their friendships, more free to speak about them. "My friend Joey . . . My friend Sheila . . ." These are introductions of a sort that pass out of speech as people grow up and follow more formal lines: "This is my boss . . ." "Professor Smith teaches anthropology." "I've wanted you to meet a business associate." Less: "Here's my best friend; I hope she'll be a friend of yours, too." Adults are not as free as that.

If friendships freely come, can they freely go? As they are born, do they die? Yes, we must admit, though not without some pain. But not everything in life needs to be clung to in the same way. One can experience the passing of some friendships without any pain at all.

If you are in your middle years, see if you can find an address book from college days or soon after, when you first embarked on adult life. I have one such worn leather-bound book, made of materials that will last for ages. It has already outlived some friendships. Scanning it, I notice that not in a single instance was a friendship killed; not in any case did

an old friend and I part as enemies. We did not even part knowing that we were parting.

Once upon a time the group of us made up "our gang." We came home from college at Christmas and partied many nights. In summer we might work six days a week, but when evening came there was always time for a date, a hamburger, or a long visit. A few score of us probably thought of each other as friends. Some disappeared for the military and never settled back home. None have the addresses they did thirty years before. Not many married within the group; as friends we had become brothers and sisters, and the attractions that cause people to marry were not strong. They tell us that so it is in the kibbutzim of Israel, where unrelated boys and girls grow up as if siblings, and choose spouses from outside their circle. So with us.

Some of the group "succeeded," and we could track them down with *Who's Who* or from people who know them. Others failed. I don't know but that some may have committed suicide though, as they say, "I should probably have heard." Once in a while when I have spoken in a faraway city someone will come up and ask, "Do you remember who I am?" And my eye retraces the outline of a face to see behind it the firmer lines of a younger face that I knew "way back when." Then it comes to me, and we spontaneously embrace. We turn to others in the circle and babble about those happy times. Everything is very genuine. We are sure that it would be nice to get together again. How are the children, if there are children? How is the spouse? Ow. Oh, I'm sorry. I hadn't heard about the divorce—or even the marriage, for that matter. And by the time I am back at the hotel and the old friend at his or her home, our meeting is only one part of the long day. Time to turn on the late-night news. A plane to catch in the morning.

To keep our sanity, we have to remember that even friends are like ships passing in the night; their lights penetrate each other's zones of visibility, their solitudes touch and greet for a while—but then they move on. The mind is not able to register nor the heart capable of storing all the positive contacts we have had through the years. We have to sort, to eliminate, to let go and let drop. There are books on my shelves that I once considered friends, books that someday will have to make room for other books. When I first read them I could not picture the day they would be part of a gift to a library or a donation to an auction. If I could regress to the high school world in which I bought them and could recreate and then freeze the moments that led me to such books, I should be a happy creature. But not necessarily a human being, for our minds are not antique shops in which we can collect literally everything.

Letting friendships fade and die, then, may be part of a natural passage or a call of God. Friends are among the earthly things that may fall with the leaves and get raked up or swept away. They may have a sweet smell, but it is like that of decaying leaves, for the odor of autumn comes with friendship. There are undying friendships, signals of resurrected life; there are dying friendships that we can restore later in life. And there are, mostly, quietly ending friendships among those far apart. Write someone a letter daily, and you cannot end the pages. Write annually, and there will be ever less to say each year.

Along the way you have used each other for advice. That brings up one more problem area in friendships: knowing the limits of the friend as a semi-professional helper. You can heed the counsel of a friend, but the friend is not a counselor. You can get therapy from a friendship, but friends are not therapists. Counselors and therapists have professional roles to fill. They become expert at what they do by years of study. Their preparation forces them to work out theories of human behavior, theories that can be of help when you present yourself and your specific problems. Through experience they have evolved comparative models by which you can locate yourself. From these few lines it should be clear that, relating to you in their professional capacity, they are highly limited human beings. You cannot capture life in roles, theories, or comparative models. That is why counselors and therapists need friends who are not their counselees or patients.

And that is why people with problems need to remember that friends cannot always be of help in every respect. Friends may be shocked at those creative moments when a therapist does not blink an eye or stop taking notes. "Doctor, I think my problems go back to the years when my father abused me sexually. You see, I . . . uh . . . uh." "Yes, go on?" The doctor has heard it before; maybe she hears it every day. That does not necessarily make you Case 306B, Category Incest. But it means that you are in a flow with which the doctor can cope. She can help you locate yourself in this flow and help you begin to face your problem.

Things are different if, out of a rather clear blue-gray sky, you unload a problem based on incest on an unsuspecting friend. This friend has never been within textbook range of theory and would not know the incest taboo from a blind date. The friend has never met anyone with your problem and finds the topic disgusting. But rather than show it, he overwhelms you with torrents of shock and sympathy, all designed to help you but all capable of covering over his inexperience and ineptness. He means well, but he does not possess the means necessary for helping you to overcome your difficulty.

The therapist—or the priest, for that matter—often plays the part of a half-impersonal "other" who represents a larger humanity to the troubled soul. Take the priest: He can put on the robes of the confessional and speak with you about the God who presides over a moral universe in which you both find acceptance. In the act of forgiveness you rejoin the human race and enjoy a new dignity. Then this same priest can step out of his robes, put on a T-shirt, and clean up on you during a few rounds of golf until you think you have no dignity left. A friend can clean up on you, but he or she is not likely to be a successful embodiment of a larger humanity that must affirm you when you do not deserve it.

To observe that the friend is not a counselor or therapist is not to freeze him out of counsel but to see his gift in a special light. Your friend probably has no more experience with your problem than you do, and can receive the shock much as you do. Together you may live with it and perhaps together you seek counsel. The therapist can say, "You are well on your way to cure; you simply have to experience the acceptance of other human beings." And your friend comes on the scene to be an agent of acceptance. The priest is enabled to say something as shocking as "God forgives you" or "I'll forgive you" before turning you loose on a world that does not seem hospitable. And the friend creates a haven of hospitality where you can regather your energies for a more open assault on less accepting portions of that world.

"Talking things over" with a friend is one of the most enjoyable and, dare we say it, *useful* features of our relations. The mental stopwatch of the professional is running all the time. The clock ticks; the hour comes to an end. The priest runs a finger along the margin and soon the ritual pages of the little black book come to the word *Amen* and the session is over. You go back into the burdening night or, worse, into the sun that forces you to blink in the face of a world that wants to do you in. But a friend, though she may be busy, is not monitoring your relation so closely. There is no next patient or next sinner waiting in the outer office or the next booth. There is, for now, only you. "Yes, I know you've told me a thousand times, but sometimes the truth comes through to me the thousand-and-first. So let's take another run at it. No, I don't know whether I can help you, but I think that my just being here with you is better than if I left you alone just now." Friendship thus finds its own distinctive place in a society where most other ties are commercial and programmed.

9

The Rites of Friendship

Friends engage each other freely and sometimes playfully. This does not mean that one can take the other captive. They both have their rights. Healthy friends also have their rites. In religion people follow certain rituals in order to ward off chaos. So it is in friendship, which draws here as so often upon the same elements in life that make us religious. Whether they are consistent and formal about the ceremonies of friendship, or whether they simply let these take casual but durable form, friends will find themselves repeating acts and rites that have cemented friendships.

Friendship is a zone in which moderns can permit ritual and tradition to play their rightful parts. In the commercial world, money dominates and firms have to reorient themselves constantly in pursuit of profit. A department store may have been in the hands of a notable family for five or six generations. But a bold entrepreneur with an impulse to take over could come up with a proposal that sticks by showing the stockholders ways in which the change might be to their advantage. The family would be out and the firm taken over. Large firms cannot be simply devoted to family tradition.

You may have settled down into a comfortable pattern in your community; perhaps you have plans to raise the children there. Then, on any March 1, you get called into the board room. "We have great confidence in you, Biggs. And to show it, we are going to put you in charge of the Birmingham branch. You will leave next month. You can be sure that we will take care of your family's moving expenses at the end of the school year. We would not want to uproot them now."

Commerce is not the only destroyer of tradition. Government can do the same. Public policy often leads to urban renewal and the destruction of neighborhood ties. Bureaucracies have to be efficient. They cannot permit a family to take care of an aging couple on welfare at little expense to the state. There is a "solution" for such couples: Move them to a home far from the rites of neighborhood and ties to friends. Sure, it will cost more. But this is more efficient.

People with complaints about such treatment are likely to get the runaround. Are you shaken up by the policy of your firm or your city? Well, we can do something about it. Professionals have been your problem? Here's your solution. You see, we pay this professional ombudsman well. He can listen to your problems and see if we can do something to lessen them. No, we can't let you stay here at the same level and pay; you have to go. No, we can't let you take care of the old Gonzalez couple in the Latino neighborhood. But the ombudsman will listen to them when we have relocated them. Here is his phone number; tell them to call any time.

It would be nice if we could walk in on that scene with a solution to the problem of impersonality. And not everyone is a victim. An ingenious public finds ways to fight back. Gifted people constantly work to find alternative ways of dealing with ties and traditions in society. For example, the hospice movement allows people with terminal disease to spend their last days in settings where someone can keep track of continuities in the lives of the dying. In retirement communities some churches work to recreate the circumstances of the old church or the old neighborhood so residents will not feel such a strong sense of being uprooted. But these are halfway measures, for the few.

Where modern life permits no solutions, it sometimes allows caring people to address problems rationally or provides means to head off the worst that impersonality can generate. One might almost call friendship nature's way of keeping traditions alive, of nourishing roots. If you charted the course of a long friendship, it is likely that you would see it as an agent of tradition. When do you sing with adults? You might mumble through the national anthem before a Dodgers game, or stumble through "Holy, Holy, Holy" at church. But otherwise you exercise your vocal cords only in the shower. Except when old friends gather.

Someone remembers the songs from the campfire back at Timberline, from high school days. And you start singing them. When your voices tire someone

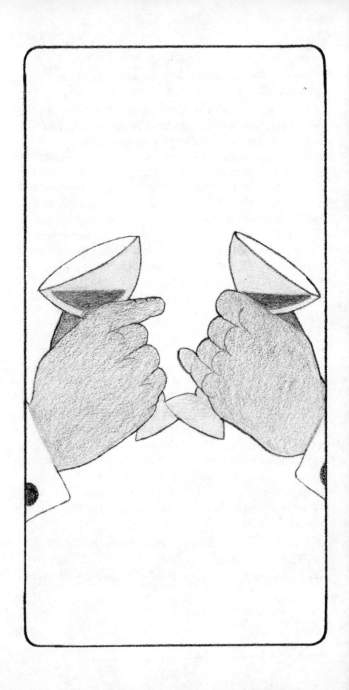

remembers that you did this last year, too, when the old gang got together. Next come the sorority songs. One of the circle starts telling stories about the pranks you played. Remember old Professor Chips? And she launches into the reminiscences. No matter that they are the same stories you heard last year. Or, rather, it *does* matter that they are the same stories. The telling of them confirms the meaning of your bonds as if it were a rite. Your child wonders why the adults he just overheard were so silly. What was funny about those stories? Why did everybody sing in the backyard? Only later will he begin to learn that these noises were signals of a ritual that no computers could suppress, no bureaus destroy.

If not song, then traditions of gift-giving and observance of special occasions serve to express and reinforce friendship in a careless world. Every year at Derby time you arrange to see Louisville again. Down at the office they think you must be an addict, "always playing the horses." Frankly, you couldn't care less who is running this year, and you probably don't know. You want to be with the Franks, whom you haven't seen since the last Derby. And you know that when you get to your motel room, Ed will have arranged for the same kind of flowers he ordered last year. At five o'clock there'll be a knock on the door, and he will be there wearing those white shoes which—he blushes as you notice—he shined up for the annual occasion. Mint juleps, anyone?

Thanksgiving Day: The kids have been gone for years, and since you see them at Christmas, the family doesn't get together for Thanksgiving. But the Morrises, who are in the same situation, invited you over for dinner seven or eight years ago, and you've been exchanging the occasion every year since. You always observe the same ritual: an hour at church. "We gather together to ask the Lord's blessing." Then to the dinner table. Time for a few long-distance calls to the children of both families. Someone mutters a word about how much all of you have to be thankful for. Harry kids as he always does that this year the men will do the dishes even though they helped make the meal, "thanks to Women's Lib," and the women wince a bit. They know that after dinner the men will not be found loading the dishwasher, but tuning in to the football game. In the evening, left-overs and cold cuts and the drive back across town. See you next year. You have retold the stories, fused your lives, affirmed your humanity. When you start forgetting, or making provision to forget, you find yourself becoming a bit less than human.

It is in the observance of rite and tradition that friendship comes closest to being a religious aspect of life. I do not mean that friendship cannot merely be friendship or that it has value only if we put it on a high shelf marked "Top Sacred." Nor do we do religion a favor by spreading its definition so thin that anything can go by that name. Instead, it is useful to see the similes and coincidences. Religion, however disruptive it can be when it judges human pretense and injustice, has another task: It helps keep stories alive and, in doing so, endows past suffering with meaning and gives hope to the present. Some people complain that religion is conservative—which it is, when it has this storytelling function. But this is a conservatism that saves what the uncaring would trample or forget at the cost of what is most humanly

precious. And religion encourages rites as a way of warding off chaos. At the edges of ritual life everything seems plotless and threatening. But when people gather to repeat what they did and said at sundown yesterday or sunup last Sunday, when they regather for Yom Kippur or Easter as they did a year ago, they give a name to the order that they must have to fight the chaos.

Friendship is not a substitute for religious ritual but a supplement to it. When worshippers return from matins in the morning, assured of grace in a new day, they lose heart if they never run into friends who act gracefully. Easter may be a celebration of new life, and the message of resurrection has the effect of forming communities now as from the beginning. But if those communities are nothing more than interest groups or address lists, the New Life message turns old and deadly. Congregants have to become friends, or at least the congregations must include friendships. And while these friendships will sometimes bring surprise based on sudden graces or unforeseen demands, they also provide for regular observance. Through old friendships we cycle ourselves back into a story that sustains life; through new friendships we set up new stories and start locating new rites. These rites serve to indicate that behind the story of our mundane lives there is a larger story. We thus endow our sufferings and joys with a meaning that tells us not everything is random and insignificant. Philosophers of the absurd may band together for a cause, as they did during the French Resistance to Nazism. But when friends start saying yes to the meaning of their rituals, they take on a pattern of affirming life and going beyond the absurd. That is why friendship not only helps reinforce vital faith but challenges weak visions.

If what you call friendship lacks common songs or stories, if there are no ritualized exchanges of gifts or holidays, if you do not find it possible to count on what your friend will do in special circumstances simply because she has done it before, you are not getting out of the relation all that great friendship promises. But ritual does not just happen. Someone has to take pains to prize it and work at it—even if playfully. And it is this playful spirit that keeps friendship from turning to idolatry in one of its great functions: support and praise.

If friendship can bring out an envy that each of us must face, it can also be a stimulant to praise. One of the most overlooked human needs is our need to be praised. That people have needs for food, sex, and security is a notion with which we are all familiar. That a child needs encouragement is apparent to any teacher who wants to bring out the best in her. If every drawing is met with an "Oh, Susan, that's not what a house looks like," Susan will soon start drawing houses that conform to everyone else's vision. She will also begin to suppress creative power and close in on herself. Why should she risk getting shot down every time her imagination has led her to perk up? A good teacher knows that to hand out gold stars and bronze trophies every day is a self-defeating exercise. But in the course of a long relation, there is room for a thousand subtle signals that tell the child she has a place. Through such signals she learns that there are reasons for trust in a universe not of her making. There will be islands of care. "You did very well today, Susan. Good. Now we better get to work and plan tomorrow. The project is a bit harder."

Some adults are open addicts for praise. They will bribe their way into the Knights of Malta or make donations to colleges that in turn award enough honorary doctorates that they almost die by degrees. The Boy Scout merit badge mentality never leaves them. Yet many Catholics love God and will serve humans whether or not someone dubs them Knights. And philanthropists find motives other than lining up for honors. They might actually believe in the cause of higher education and take quiet delight in seeing unthinking collegians make use of scholarships whose source they never heard of. Such people will not necessarily shrink from recognition, but they do not need it as regularly as a fix.

Because many gifted adults live such full lives that the need for being praised is not obvious, and because many others are so seldom praised that they dare hardly get their expectations up, people forget that it is not only children who need to be affirmed. Friendship, by the consent of almost all who reflect on it, is a sphere in which praise can live without becoming overbearing. "Nag, nag, nag" a friend and the friend is likely to drift off. "Praise, praise, praise" a friend and he is likely to become suspicious. Friends do not have to denounce each other ritually or praise each other through ceremonial provision. But because they can take for granted the lows and highs of a relation, they may neglect the highs.

The friend is a credible person from whom to accept praise, although most of us would tend to weary of a relation based solely on flattery. A friend may be blind to your faults; that is one hazard. But the friend has also learned better than has the boss or the teacher what your limits are. So, curiously, praise from a friend may often have a measure of objectivity. If you play your flute for a friend who insists that you are as good as Jean-Pierre Rampal, unless you are in fact that good, you should have enough sense to think less of him. His taste is uninformed or his motive is suspect.

If I tell you that the new sweater you have knitted is better than anything I have seen from you, it is likely to be true. Of course, there is always the danger that if I admire it, you will give it to me and I will have to wear it. If I like the way you are doing your hair now and say so, it had better be true—if you care about my opinion you are likely to keep wearing it that way for some time, in part to please me and in part because you have taken my word for it. And if my word was flattery, I will have to suffer through months of seeing one of my friends at less than her best. If I compliment you without a word over the way the two of us have grown together in the art of friendship, you will know, and act upon the knowledge. If I give the wrong signal, you are likely to nurture those very aspects of our friendship that I find cloying or embarrassing.

Here again we find a simile between friendship and the way biblical faith pictures divine-human ties. We do not begin with the portrayal of God as a friend who praises us. The idolatry of the human is abhorred in biblical witness. We do not become praiseworthy and thus earn the friendship of God. But after the transaction of grace occurs—or apart from that transaction, when we are not in the act of pleasing or appeasing God—we experience acts of encouragement. Call it praise from God. You have been given a name; the very hairs of your head are all numbered. God cares more for you than for the lilies of the field or the birds of the air, and in some contexts they are doing pretty well, aren't they? Then why do you worry, you of "little faith?"? Perhaps these words do not sound much like praise by God, since their tone is scolding. Read another way, however, we can see these words as a basis for affirmation. You are valuable. It belongs to the nature of the case that you are to be cared for and about.

If the human is valuable as part of creation, a person takes on distinctive worth as a member of the New Creation, the world in which the risen Christ touches everything with possibility. And here even those writers who make most of making least about their own efforts have to recognize the value of growth in grace. The same Paul who "counts as dung" his own achievements knows that if one is bonded to God inwardly, "his praise is not from men but from God" (Romans 2:29).

To know the praise of God is to know a liberating experience that frees humans from the necessity of asking themselves every day, "How am I doing?" Thus freed, they can begin to notice the neighbor. So it is with friendship. If you button up and never let one friend know that he is intrinsically valuable, or that another's attitudes lead you to affirm her, they will be preoccupied. Are they doing something wrong? What would it take to please you? But the occasional gesture or, even better, the explicit word of encouraging praise, frees them for other things. They do not have to be obsessed with caring for the

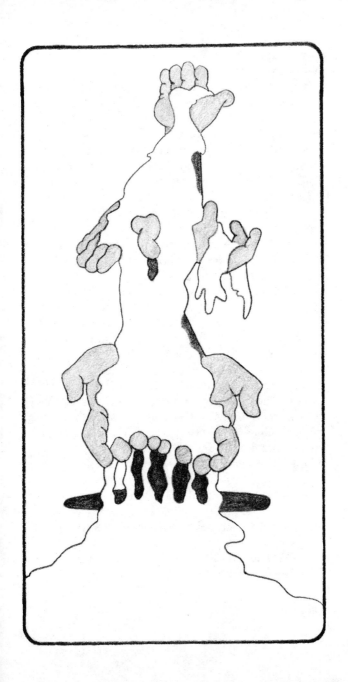

friend and can give time without care for the sake of the otherwise friendless.

I hope that our conversation on friendship has not been too clubby. There is a danger that a chat in a library that surrounds us with books offering clues to friendship might encourage only one set of interpretations and blind us to other meanings. Here as so often I have to plead in the line of Jean-Jacques Rousseau: You can expect my thoughts to be consistent with each other, but you cannot expect me to assert them all at the same time. So this book did not find us saying much about the poor of the world, or the great problem associated with what humans are doing to their environment, or the threat people pose to each other in the face of war.

That does not mean that friendship does not link up with those other themes. While there is a danger that it can lead people to build cocoons of exclusivity around themselves, being friends is still one of the best non-governmental and low-budget ways of preparing for relations in the larger world. People who move with the invincible security that comes with trusting and being trusted can use the justice they have learned in their own friendly relations to assert similar values away from home. The acts of generosity that nurture friendship can turn beyond two people who act reciprocally. They can learn to see through the eyes of people who never experience generosity. So friendship, as a gift of God for the sorrowing creatures to give them a joy worthy of their destiny, becomes an incentive to carry on the works of God in that world of sorrows. That is a bonus, a final gift that comes with friendship. It is far from being among the least.